Palgrave Studies in Classical Liberalism

Series Editors

David F. Hardwick, Department of Pathology and Laboratory Medicine, The University of British Columbia, Vancouver, BC, Canada

Leslie Marsh, Department of Economics, Philosophy and Political Science, The University of British Columbia, Okanagan, BC, Canada

This series offers a forum to writers concerned that the central presuppositions of the liberal tradition have been severely corroded, neglected, or misappropriated by overly rationalistic and constructivist approaches.

The hardest-won achievement of the liberal tradition has been the wrestling of epistemic independence from overwhelming concentrations of power, monopolies and capricious zealotries. The very precondition of knowledge is the exploitation of the epistemic virtues accorded by society's situated and distributed manifold of spontaneous orders, the DNA of the modern civil condition.

With the confluence of interest in situated and distributed liberalism emanating from the Scottish tradition, Austrian and behavioral economics, non-Cartesian philosophy and moral psychology, the editors are soliciting proposals that speak to this multidisciplinary constituency. Sole or joint authorship submissions are welcome as are edited collections, broadly theoretical or topical in nature.

Lesley A. Jacobs · Matthew McManus

Against Post-Liberal Courts and Justice

Rescuing Ronald Dworkin's Legacy

Lesley A. Jacobs
Ontario Tech University & York
University
Toronto, ON, Canada

Matthew McManus
Department of Political Science
University of Michigan–Ann Arbor
Ann Arbor, MI, USA

ISSN 2662-6470 ISSN 2662-6489 (electronic)
Palgrave Studies in Classical Liberalism
ISBN 978-3-031-45346-5 ISBN 978-3-031-45347-2 (eBook)
https://doi.org/10.1007/978-3-031-45347-2

Cover credit: Pattadis Walarput/Alamy Stock Photo

This Palgrave Macmillan imprint is published by the registered company Springer Nature Switzerland AG
The registered company address is: Gewerbestrasse 11, 6330 Cham, Switzerland

Paper in this product is recyclable.

Dedicated to our families

ACKNOWLEDGMENTS

Any book naturally accrues more debts than could ever be acknowledged. This factors exponentially when it is co-authored. Rather than go on for dozens of pages we'd just like to single out the most singular influences. Firstly thanks to York University, Ontario Tech University, and the University of Michigan for their ongoing support. This is especially true of the administrators and custodians who kept the world running in the midst of an unprecedented pandemic. And of course thanks to the faculty and staff in York's Department of Social Science, especially the graduate program in socio-legal studies. It has grown an awful lot since the authors met in 2011 and that is something to be proud of. Secondly, thank you to Dr. Leslie Marsh and the editors of Palgrave's ongoing series on the liberal tradition and its discontents. Their encouragement and enthusiasm for this little book, and for that matter liberalism as a whole, is infectious and necessary. Thirdly, thank you to Professor Ronald Dworkin for your mentorship, and may you rest in peace. Legal and political philosophy lost an irreplaceable titan when you passed in 2013. Hopefully, this book does some justice to such a rich and sweeping legacy. And last, but not at least, thank you to our extended families and friends. Any merits the book may have are due to you far more than to the authors. Of course, the faults rest exclusively on our shoulders. That's how it should be.

CONTENTS

CHAPTER 1

Introduction

Abstract This introductory chapter summarizes the main approach to
the book and makes the case for Ronald Dworkin's relevance in the
twenty-first century. It discusses the main arguments of each Chapter,
gesturing the major cases and themes that will be discussed. The chapter
concludes with an explanation for why Ronald Dworkin is the legal theorist and philosopher liberals need to combat the influence of post-liberal
authoritarianism in law and politics.

Keyword Post-liberal justice · Analytical jurisprudence · Trumpism

REINTRODUCING RONALD DWORKIN

Cultures have tried to teach a malign and apparently persuasive lie: that the
most important metric of a good life is wealth and the luxury and power
it brings. The rich think they live better when they are even richer. In
America and many other places they use their wealth politically, to persuade
the public to elect or accept leaders who will do that for them. They say
that the justice we have imagined is socialism that threatens our freedom.
Not everyone is gullible: many people lead contented lives without wealth.
But many others are persuaded; they vote for low taxes to keep the jackpot

© The Author(s), under exclusive license to Springer Nature
Switzerland AG 2023
L. A. Jacobs and M. McManus, *Against Post-Liberal Courts and Justice*,
Palgrave Studies in Classical Liberalism,
https://doi.org/10.1007/978-3-031-45347-2_1

full in case they too can win it, even though that is a lottery they are almost bound to lose. Nothing better illustrates the tragedy of an unexamined life: there are no winners in this macabre dance of greed and delusion. No respectable or even intelligible theory of value supposes that making and spending money has any value or importance in itself and almost everything people buy with that money lacks any importance as well. The ridiculous dream of a princely life is kept alive by ethical sleepwalkers. And they in turn keep injustice alive because their self-contempt breeds a politics of contempt for others. Dignity is indivisible.

Ronald Dworkin, *Justice for Hedgehogs (2011).*

In the 1990s, it looked as though liberal institutions—constitutional democracy, economic markets, liberal courts, free trade, international human rights—had triumphed so completely over its rivals that some pundits could plausibly argue we'd reached the end of history. A quarter century later no one believes that. Liberal democracies appear to have weathered the worst of the conservative authoritarian and far right populist storm that began brewing in 2008 and reached hurricane pitch by 2018. But there is no guarantee we're not resting in the eye of a storm that will spin back round to rip us apart. At its climax most major countries on earth—India, Brazil, United States, Russia, Italy, Turkey—were governed by a right populist transparent in their contempt for liberalism. Britain and France weren't far behind, and many felt that autocratic "illiberal democracies" like Hungary and Poland might rip up the European Union as a stepping stone to eroding the international order.

Accompanying this dramatic transition was a wave of intellectual efforts by conservative and far right thinkers. They went by many different names: national conservatives, illiberal democrats, traditionalists, neoreactionaries, identitarians, and Christian nationalists. All were united in their conviction that we'd entered, or needed to enter, an era of post-liberal institutions. Some of the most sophisticated even adopted this as a nom de clef whose futurist quality didn't hide their reactionary intentions. While the emotional and political demands of these right-wing critics were very different, they shared a core conviction that liberalism was patently unjust. Liberalism was too nihilistic, too individualistic, too libertine, not really libertine enough (especially on free speech rights for the political right), too egalitarian, too cosmopolitan, too elitist, not elitist enough, too individualistic to be anything good. For all these reasons and plenty more, the post-liberals and their allies held that liberalism needed to go the way of the dodo.

In many ways, American liberal institutions deserved the hate. For half a century, liberals had either aligned or resigned themselves to one of the most pitiless economic projects in recent memory. The labor movement was all but broken, the social democratic dream of making the boons of liberalism available to all had stalled or was in retreat, and many people of color saw little movement on actually making Dr. King's dream of a post-racist society a reality. Empirically minded analysts like Eatwell and Goodwin confirmed that a burgeoning number of citizens felt that political elites held them in little regard and were convinced that liberal democratic institutions were unresponsive to their needs while being slavishly responsive to the rich.[1] Worse, Martin Gilens[2] and Thomas Piketty provided evidence that citizens were right to feel that way-a fact compounded by uniquely bad court decisions like *Citizens United*.[3] And when confronted with surging illiberalism how did many liberal elites respond? By publishing sighing op-eds in elite media venues with charming titles like "Its Time For the Elites to Rise Up Against the Ignorant Masses."[4]

What liberals needed was to rediscover or reinvent two essential qualities of liberalism from the past. The first was to reconnect with the principled basis of liberalism in defense of moral equality and dignified freedom for all. For two centuries the force of liberty, equality and their forgotten sibling fraternity were strong enough to carry all before them. And yet in the past 50 years, even as liberal institutions nominally spread, there were good reasons for citizens in liberal democracies to regard themselves as less equal, less free, and absolutely in less solidarity with other citizens. This brings us to the second quality, which is to rediscover liberalism's patented capacity for rejuvenation by reinvention. At its best this has meant liberal institutions have transformed themselves precisely

---

[1] See Roger Eatwell and Matthew Goodwin. *National Populism and the Revolt Against Liberal Democracy* (London, UK: Penguin Books, 2018).

[2] Martin Gilens and Benjamin I Page. "Testing Theories of American Politics: Elites, Interests Groups, and Average Citizens." *Perspectives on Politics*, Vol 12, 2014 and Thomas Piketty. *Capital and Ideology*, trans. Arthur Goldhammer. (Cambridge, MA: Harvard University Press, 2020).

[3] Thomas Piketty. *Capital and Ideology*, trans. Arthur Goldhammer. (Cambridge, MA: Harvard University Press, 2020).

[4] See James Traub. "Its Time For The Elites To Rise Up Against The Ignorant Masses." *Foreign Policy*, June 28th 2016.

by becoming more integrally dedicated to core principles; whether that be through an extension of basic rights to women and people of color, sexual liberation, the partial strides towards economic justice taken by the mid-century social democracies, or the growing awareness of the urgency of global justice.

Few have done more to demonstrate the power of liberal rejuvenation through reinvention than Ronald Dworkin. He had little patience for liberal defeatism or liberal triumphalism, seeing both as reflective of stagnation. From *Taking Rights Seriously* through to *Justice For Hedgehogs,* Dworkin in a series of books has insisted that a liberal world view integrally committed to its moral principles had to be active in bringing about a more just social order. This would include through a muscular program of legal activism, economic redistribution, and of course empowering the basic rights of all liberal citizens. But we worry that in the public sphere Dworkin's contributions have become forgotten or, even worse, misappropriated by those who advance post-liberal institutions. This book seeks to rescue Dworkin's legacy to make the case against post-liberal courts and justice. We argue in this book that Dworkin's insights in jurisprudence as well as moral and political theory offer us a glimpse into the past not realized to point us in the direction of a better future. Although there continues to be a steady stream of scholarship by academics that addresses his work, what has been missing for the past decade is Dworkin's powerful voice as a public intellectual who readily engaged in current affairs, challenging unjust policies and poor judicial decisions. This short, punchy book is designed to reinsert Dworkin's voice into public conversations about post-liberal institutions and their intellectual foundations.

Dworkin spent his entire sixty-year career providing regular public commentary on cases before the Supreme Court of the United States. Following his lead, the insights we offer in individual chapters in this book are concretely illustrated by focusing on some of the most controversial recent post-liberal decisions of the Supreme Court. In many respects, the actions and decisions of the Supreme Court today exemplify what we can expect from post-liberal courts. Those decisions include major reversals on safeguards for democratic elections (Citizens United & Rucho v Common), abortion rights (Dobbs), race-based affirmative action (Students for Fair Admissions v. Harvard & UNC), and affordable access to universities and colleges (Biden v. Nebraska). We harvest Dworkin's thinking to formulate both our case against post-liberal courts and justice and a compelling vision of an alternative to post-liberal legal and political institutions.

Against Post-Liberal Courts and Justice: Reinventing Ronald Dworkin consists of seven chapters. This chapter introduces the book's themes and summarizes its contents. Chapter 2 will provide a brief biography and historical contextualization of Dworkin's life and work. The biographical material will foreground the influence of mentors like US Supreme Court Justice Learned Hand and the philosophers H.L.A Hart and John Rawls on Dworkinian theory. We will also discuss Dworkin's profound interest with, and engagement in, the great political disputes of the day. This includes the controversies surrounding civil rights and racial justice, the liberal Warren Court, and Dworkin's growing disillusionment with the SCOTUS after the initiation of its conservative turn in the 1980s. Chapter 2 will provide a succinct introduction to Dworkin's mature legal and political philosophy, tracing its evolution from 1977's *Taking Rights Seriously* to the 2011 publication of *Justice for Hedgehogs*. Our intention is to be as non-technical and clear as possible, while stressing the deep continuities Dworkin himself highlighted across his writings. We will begin with a discussion of his seminal critique of legal positivism and definition of rights as "trumps," before moving on to analyzing Dworkin's account of "law as integrity" and his description of how Judges should interpret the law. The chapter will then conclude with a brief discussion of Dworkin's liberal egalitarian political philosophy, stressing the importance he placed on an ideal of the rule as law grounded on "equal respect and concern" for its members, and that this requires a commitment to a kind of equality of resources.

Chapter 3 will discuss Dworkin's account of constitutional democracy and the role he thought Courts should play in a liberal society. This will lean heavily on his books *Law's Integrity* and *Freedom's Law: A Moral Reading of the American Constitution*. We will discuss both his rejection of the Originalist idea that any "moral reading" of law entails Judges usurping democratic powers for themselves, and his argument that the fact that Judges must make complex moral judgments isn't necessarily undemocratic. We will argue that Dworkin is undoubtedly open to accusations of elitism and even having a naïve faith in Judges, based on a lionization of the Warren Court which is unrepresentative of the largely reactionary role SCOTUS has played through American history.

Never the less, liberals and democrats should both be deeply attentive to Dworkin's insistence that democracy must entail more than mere majority rule. Instead, it is predicated on the principle of paying equal respect to all citizens on the basis of their being dignified and free beings. This requires not only affirming an expansive collection of rights to citizens but also being proactive in rectifying forms of injustice and inequities of power which would result in the law paying unequal respect to different individuals. Understood properly this requires Courts to do what they can to expand democratic opportunities for citizens and ensure they enjoy equal value from their political liberties. One example of this can be found in Dworkin's scathing critique of the *Citizens United* decision on the basis that it makes citizens patently unequal in the political process.

Chapter 4 will focus on racial integration and affirmative action, anchored in the legacy of the 1954 *Brown v. Board of Education* case. We will foreground how Dworkin considered himself a firm defender of racial justice, which included defending race-based affirmative action programs even when they became subject to wide criticism by conservatives and not few liberals on the basis that the violated the Equal Protections Clause in the constitution as well as the 1964 *Civil Rights Act*. Affirmative action and other ameliorative programmes are framed by Dworkin as forward looking and delivering important societal benefits, rather than focused on history and compensation. This framing reveals the shortcomings and weaknesses of Chief Justice Robert's majority opinion in *Students for Fair Admissions Inc. v. President and Fellows of Harvard College* and *Students for Fair Admissions Inc. v. University of North Carolina, the two 2023 cases where the Supreme Court reversed its fifty-year holding that race-sensitive admissions decisions were constitutional.*

Chapter 5 will discuss Dworkin's approach to life-and-death issues such as abortion and euthanasia. While many liberals hoped these would be settled controversies, the resurgent populist right and its post-liberal defenders have gotten increasingly ambitious in challenging socially liberal policies and seeking a return to conservative moralism. This was spectacularly seen in the repeal of *Roe vs Wade* by the US Supreme Court in the Dobbs case. In these contexts, it is important to ask why liberal egalitarians should be committed to social progressivism and inclusion.

Dworkin's critique of social conservatism has deep roots; going as far back as his scathingly critical response to Lord Patrick Devlin's defense of the criminalization of homosexuality.[5] He tends to frame his defense

---

[5] Ronald Dworkin. "Lord Devlin and the Enforcement of Morals" *The Yale Law Journal*, Vol 75, No 6, 1966.

of homosexuality in terms of individual rights, and we will argue that his liberal position organically extends to upholding the rights of trans persons too. More complicated are Dworkin's arguments about pornography and abortion, since he acknowledges the force of radical feminist critiques of pornography on the one hand and anxieties about the rights of the unborn on the other. His defense of pornography as expression and his support for abortion flow from much the same place. He believes that constitutionally individuals are recognized by the law as having certain fundamental rights, which entitle them to engage in acts that may be ethically frowned upon and perhaps even politically corrosive. This is because in his view a proper reading of the First and Fourteenth Amendments recognizes their complementarity and the fact that the freedom to express one's self flows from the commitment to equal protection. By contrast, Dworkin argues that the abortion debate is a non-starter since even though a fetus clearly is "life" of a certain sort, it is not life which is granted any recognizable—let alone equal—protection by constitutional law; a fetus lacks interests of the sort American constitutional law gives moral weight. This is a very novel way of conceptualizing the liberal commitment to both freedom and equality in the law which is distinctly Dworkinian in its reasoning. We will defend his position on these issues, arguing Dworkin provides an argument to the effect that respecting the freedom and equality of citizens requires a liberal approach to law, and decisively precludes implementing socially conservative policies.

Chapter 6 discusses Dworkin's arguments for what he calls Equality of Resources, within the context of the American Dream and Equality of Opportunity. The American Dream is the familiar and quintessential promise that anyone, regardless of his or her origins, can have a fair start in life in a liberal society. If we work hard, we can get a good education and achieve success. For Dworkin, this promise flows from the long-standing liberal commitment to the dignity and autonomy of the individual. Positioned as a novel account of the fairness required by equality of opportunity, equality of resources balances two basic principles, one is that liberal institutions should ensure that people's fates or life chances are insensitive to their familial background, race or gender, the other principle is that a person's life prospects are shaped by the choices they make and their personal responsibility for making those choices. Attending college or university is one of the key ladders for realizing the American Dream. Recent decisions by the US Supreme Court to curtail initiatives such as comprehensive post-secondary student debt relief suggest that post-liberal institutions are winning on any commitment to the American Dream and equality of opportunity. Dworkinian equality of resources offers robust but nuanced insights into why initiatives like student relief are needed to secure equal opportunity for all.

Chapter 7 will conclude the book with a discussion of our post-liberal moment for courts and the justice system, focusing in particular on the writings of Patrick Deneen and Adrian Vermeule. The latter will be especially important, and we will discuss and rebut Vermeule's reactionary reinterpretation of Dworkinian jurisprudence in his recent *Common Good Constitutionalism*. In this book Vermeule agrees with Dworkin that any approach to the law must invariably be moral but goes on to defend a socially conservative integralist model which owes more to Carl Schmitt and even Joseph de Maistre than the great liberal egalitarian. We will highlight how this move raises the stakes in the debate between liberals and progressives against their conservative and post-liberal critics and showcases the need for a thought leader like Dworkin who can teach us how to defend a muscular approach to law committed to freedom and equality. *Against Post-Liberal Courts and Justice* ends on a positive note, calling for liberals and progressives to reacquaint themselves with Dworkin's work as we move deeper into an agonistic political universe.

CHAPTER 2

Ronald Dworkin's Legacy

Abstract This chapter reevaluates the scope of Ronald Dworkin's contributions to law, legal theory, and political philosophy. It offers a quick biography of his life and life's work, before summarizing some of the core ideas that constitute his enduring intellectual legacy. This chapter also foregrounds some of the objectionable features of Dworkinean thinking we will address more substantively later in the book.

Keyword Legal positivism · Law as Integrity · The Semantic Sting · The Unity of Value

DWORKIN'S LIFE AND CAREER

Dworkin was fond of a parable bequeathed by his mentor Justice Learned Hand. The no doubt very learned Justice Learned Hand turns to Dworkin and asks if he'd like to learn about heaven. Dworkin responds that he'd be eternally grateful. After ascending to well-deserved bliss in heaven Hand gets to spend his time relaxing with the great intellects of the past. The conversation flowed as liberally as the exceptionally dry martinis. Epigram followed epigram in a crescendo of wit and elegance until someone finally said "Shut up Voltaire. I want to hear what Hand

L. A. Jacobs and M. McManus, *Against Post-Liberal Courts and Justice*, Palgrave Studies in Classical Liberalism, https://doi.org/10.1007/978-3-031-45347-2_2

is saying."[1] This anecdote was quintessential Dworkin. Polished, suave, and erudite. Gently undercutting its own pomp at just the right moment with dry wit. More than a little bourgeois, but always honestly expressing joy at mentorship and companionship. And—above all else—warm and optimistic in its gratitude for the good life.

Ronald Myles Dworkin was born in 1931 into a lower middle-class Jewish family in Rhode Island. He died in London on February 14, 2013, at the age of 81. His parents separated when he was quite young, and his mother worked as a music teacher to support herself and her children. A prodigiously talented student, Dworkin won a scholarship to Harvard where he breezed through a tough curriculum with style. This won Dworkin a Rhodes Scholarship, which he used to read law at Oxford University. Dworkin embarked on a legal career that included clerking for Justice Hand. He quickly moved on from normal legal work, and decided his time was better spent in academia. For much of the rest of his life, Dworkin's time would be divided between Britain and the United States, as he assumed a variety of academic appointments in each country's top universities. At the same, he assumed the role of being a major public intellectual, serving as a regular contributor to The *New York Review of Books* which provided a forum for frequent interventions into current affairs of the day. Our book is designed as an intervention on pressing issues today, much in the same spirit as Dworkin exemplified as a public intellectual.

Like many academics, the most exciting parts of Dworkin's biography so far as the public should be concerned are his writings. From that standpoint 1977 was the most important professional year in Dworkin's life, since it marked the publication of his seminal book *Taking Rights Seriously*. We'll discuss both the nature and impact of *Taking Rights Seriously* later, but needless to say, it made a nuclear splash upon publication. Dworkin was almost immediately hailed as one of the Anglo-American world's leading philosophers of law, and luminaries like Hart felt compelled to write defensive rebuttals of till-then dominant legal positivism.[2] Intellectually the book didn't disappoint, sketching out a very

---

[1] See Ronald Dworkin. "Is There Truth In Interpretation? Law, Literature, and History." *Library of Congress,* December 17th, 2009 at https://www.youtube.com/watch?v=742JyiqLhuk.

[2] See the Postscript to H.L.A. Hart *The Concept of Law: Second Edition.* (Oxford, UK: Oxford University Press, 1997).

novel critique of legal positivism ala Austin and Hart. While at the same time defending a view of the law that took rights more seriously than just about anyone else.

Saying all that, unlike Hart, John Rawls, or John Finnis, it would be misleading to say that *Taking Rights Seriously* contains more or less the germ of every other significant contribution Dworkin made. Dworkin's most comprehensive and best book on legal theory, *Law's Empire*, was published in 1986. Building on the promise of *Taking Rights Seriously*, *Law's Empire* laid out a unified field theory of law as integrity, legal interpretation, rights, and left-liberal political philosophy. It also offered far and away the sharpest critique of the view that law and legal disputes can be reduced to linguistic or "semantic" debates about the meaning of words, as Dworkin's ascendent originalist rivals were keen to argue. Much of this built upon the early critique of legal positivism, which conceived of law along the lines of a "model of rules." But it raised the stakes (and temperature) of Dworkin's analysis considerably. He was now not just arguing technical legal questions with fellow liberals like Hart, but diving into the grand political and moral disputes of the era. This would take him to new heights as a public intellectual, though undoubtedly one with a tragic streak.

For his entire life Dworkin identified with the muscular progressive liberalism of F.D.R, the Warren Court, the 1960s Civil Rights movement, and more globally the Human Rights Revolution. Rather like his contemporary Sheldon Wolin,[3] Dworkin's mature tone expressed no small amount of bafflement and disappointment toward the stupendous rise of legal and political conservatism through the 1980s. Unfortunately, this meant that, while *Law's Empire* and subsequent books like *Freedom's Law: A Moral Reading of the American Constitution* were enthusiastically received by scholars, the zeitgeist out of which their spirit emerged was floundering. Judges on the Supreme Court like Earl Warren and Thurgood Marshall were replaced by Antonin Scalia, Clarence Thomas, and Clarence Thomas' Patreon account. The broader political consensus of

---

[3] In his essay "The Destructive Sixties and Postmodern Conservatism" Wolin claimed "About a half century ago conservatism was little more than a crotchety defense of what used to be called vested interests, or a distaste for New Deal "leveling." Or a fondness for tasteless jokes about Franklin and Eleanor, or the affectation of English cultural ways....No longer a curiosity or an anachronism, conservatism has been made over into the opposite of its former stodgy self." See Sheldon Wolin. *Fugitive Democracy and Other Essays.* (Princeton, NJ: Princeton University Press, 2016) at pg 330.

the New Deal era broke down as Reaganism and Thatcherism emerged smoothly and assuredly as political hegemony by the late 1980s.

Not one to back down from a disagreement, Dworkin readily engaged the leading conservative jurists of his age, from Robert Bork to Richard Posner to Antonin Scalia. Dworkin opened his discussion of Antonin Scalia's textualism with the droll observation that the conservative Justice had developed an "originalist" theory of law and interpretation focused on texts and words while apparently not bothering to learn anything about the philosophy of language. Common sense would do in place of Wittgenstein or Kripke.[4] As we'll see, years later the very conservative academic Adrian Vermeule noted that Dworkin's objections to originalism were and are lethal and unanswerable by originalists.[5] They also constituted some of the most brilliant examples of Dworkin's literary style. But that mattered little to the financiers of the Federalist Society, who largely won in their long march to champion originalism. By 2010 even Elena Kagan, a progressive Obama appointee to the Supreme Court, could quip that "we are all originalists." Near the end of his life Dworkin began to express reservations that the increasingly conservative Supreme Court would never align itself with the cause of liberal justice, and even started characterizing its decisions as a threat to democracy.[6]

One might have expected from this that Dworkin would gravitate leftward, finding common ground with the counter-movements embodied by critical legal theory and is subsequent offshoots as critical feminist theory, critical race theory, queer theory, socio-legal studies and many more. And, as we'll show, in terms of his substantive convictions Dworkin was often aligned with the (often theoretically implicit) goals of critical movements and should have done far more to learn from their critiques of power and privilege. But he never reconciled himself to the critical legal movement's attraction to increasingly hip forms of structural and post-structural skepticism, and Dworkin engaged in less acerbic but equally strident debates with critical legal theorists and radical anti-liberal feminists like Catherine

---

[4] Antonin Scalia. *A Matter of Interpretation: Federal Courts and the Law.* (Princeton, NJ: Princeton Paperbacks, 1997) at pg 115.

[5] Adrian Vermeule. *Common Good Constitutionalism: Recovering the Classical Legal Tradition.* (Cambridge, UK: Polity Press, 2022).

[6] Ronald Dworkin. "The Decision That Threatens Democracy." *New York Review of Books,* May 13, 2010.

MacKinnon.[7] He often described them as lacking confidence, and as we'll explore there is some basis to Dworkin's argument that, by largely abandoning commitments to substantive moral views in favor of pure "trashing"[8] progressive and radical legal theorists did themselves a disservice. Say what you will about Scalia and Finnis, but it is undeniable that in between thinking deeply about what consenting adults were doing with their genitals at any given moment, they did have deep convictions about how much fun it was to throw black men into jail. Progressive jurists needed, in Dworkin's view, to have even firmer convictions about what legitimate courts do and say about justice.

Beyond these important debates Dworkin's last few decades were divided between weighing in on the substantial moral issues of the day in short, delightful books like *Life's Dominion: An Argument about Abortion, Euthanasia and Individual Freedom* and writing ever longer and weightier philosophical tomes like *Sovereign Virtue: The Theory and Practice of Equality.* In 2011 Dworkin published his long anticipated *Justice for Hedgehogs;* a droll title referring to Isaiah Berlin's quip that the fox knows many things, but the hedgehog knows one thing exceptionally well.

A book of staggering ambition of the sort that is rarely attempted anymore, *Justice for Hedgehogs* was released with considerable pomp and ceremony but no small amount of wariness and even skepticism. Undoubtedly Richard Mullender spoke for many in his review when claiming "Dworkin's unconvincing argument for the unity of value prompts the conclusion that, ultimately, he was not the philosopher of the American Century that he might have aspired to be. For he was unable to point the way to an end-state in which legal and other institutions ideally realize liberty, equality and other sources of positive value. Moreover, the chapter in Justice for Hedgehogs on law and morality engenders the impression that Dworkin senses that this may be the case."[9] Perhaps

---

[7] Ronald Dworkin. *Freedom's Law: The Moral Reading of the American Constitution* (Cambridge, MA: Harvard University Press, 1997) and Ronald Dworkin. "Objectivity and Truth: You'd Better Believe It." *Philosophy and Public Affairs,* Vol 25, 1996. The more critical legal minded weren't afraid of hitting back. See Allan Hutchinson. "Indiana Dworkin and Law's Empire." *Yale Law Journal,* Vol 96, 1987 and Catherine MacKinnon and Ronald Dworkin. "Pornography-An Exchange." *New York Review of Books,* October 21st, 1993.

[8] See M.G Kelman. "Trashing." *Stanford Law Review,* Vol 36, 1984.

[9] Richard Mullender. "Ronald Dworkin: Justice for Hedgehogs." *Philosophy in Review,* XXXIV, 2014 at pg 221.

it's the case that no book trying to argue for something as ambitious as the unity of all value could ever live up to its goals. But, as we'll see, there are treasures to be found in *Justice for Hedgehogs* which have not yet been claimed. The book stands as both the fullest and clunkiest exposition of Dworkin's entire philosophy.

DISCUSSING KEY DWORKINIAN CONCEPTS

Dworkin once distinguished two ways of connecting theory and practice. One was moving from the "outside in" where an author constructed "general theories of justice or personal ethics of constitutional interpretation from general assumptions about human nature or the structure of language or thought...and then [tries] to apply those general principles to concrete problems." As *Law's Empire* and *Justice for Hedgehogs* prove, Dworkin could push out dense, forbidding tones moving from the "outside in" with the best of them. But he was at his best engaging theory from the "opposite direction, from the inside out" where one begins with "practical problems, like the question of whether the law should ever permit abortion or euthanasia, and if so in which circumstances, and then ask which general philosophical or theoretical issues we must confront in order to resolve those practical problems."[10] Dworkin's thinking truly lived and breathed when engaging theory from the inside out, and it's also where the lived stakes of analysis really come to the fore in a way they rarely do in hard-core Oxbridge philosophy.

But it's quite difficult to get a sense of what made Dworkinean's "inside out" analysis original and piercing in the wild without understanding some of his major philosophical contributions in their most unadulterated form. So over the next few pages we'll (very briefly) introduce some of his core concepts: two critical, and three constructive. This will hopefully provide a road map for Dworkin's thinking that will be useful for the uninitiated going forward. Better yet, it might encourage readers unfamiliar with Dworkin to pick up his brick-sized volumes and realize they're not as scary as might appear. After this hazing ritual, we can move onto the more blood and guts debates that form the throbbing heart of moral, legal, and political analysis in liberal societies.

---

[10] Ronald Dworkin. *Life's Dominion: An Argument About Abortion, Euthanasia, and Individual Freedom.* (New York, NY: Vintage Books, 1994) at pg 29.

KEY DWORKINIAN CONCEPT
ONE: "THE SEMANTIC STING"

One of Dworkin's major contentions is against the idea that the study of law is primarily a study of legal language. For those who think of law in terms of its implications and consequences, this might appear common-sensical. But for those who understand law—as many of us do—as a collection of "rules" or "norms" or "commands" or "texts" it might seem equally commonsensical to think that law is about little else but language. This is especially the case in the Anglo-American world where legal posi-tivism has been the reigning shop-philosophy of law schools for a long time, with natural law and other more eccentric theories bordering on counter-cultural movements across the legal profession. This is because legal positivism, by conceiving of law as rules, norms, commands, or more recently ways of conceiving and implementing "plans,[11]" tends to reify the concept of law at the linguistic level.

Dworkin began his career well after the "linguistic turn" came to domi-nate philosophy departments across the English-speaking world. This began in the writings of logical positivists like Bertrand Russell, the early Wittgenstein, and A.J Ayer who insisted that the only statements which made "sense" were those which-appropriately enough-hooked onto the objects or facts of sense. Anything else, including potentially all moral, aesthetic, and religious statements, were literally "nonsense."[12] Later on, this very rigid understanding of language gave way to the more natu-ralistic and even psycho-anthropological approach of ordinary language philosophy. This stressed how we can effectively "dissolve" long-standing philosophical puzzles by giving them a linguistic treatment and showing how the words are used in everyday life. Rather than asking "what is justice?" or "what is the good life?" at the icy level of analytical heaven,

---

[11] Scott Shapiro. *Legality*. (Cambridge, MA: Belknap Press of Harvard University Press, 2011).

[12] The early Wittgenstein inspired many of these views, though in fact he argued that since logical description of the world could not make statements about what mattered this demonstrated the impotence of philosophy to answer the meaningful riddles about human life. The answers lay instead in existentially minded religious authors like Kierkegaard, Tolstoy, and Dostoevsky.

we'd look at the way ordinary people apply terms like justice and good-ness in writing or dialogue.[13] This had the useful effect of clearing out some of the abstractions which previous philosophers found rather addicting. But it also had the— sometimes intentional—effect of deflating what most of us take to be very serious questions that can't just be therapeutically dissolved. Derek Parfit relayed a telling story about R.M Hare, a major moral philosopher impressed by linguistic analysis. A young student told Hare that he was concerned with the meaning of life, or what "mattered." Hare carefully told him that there was no way a general exis-tential question about "what matters" could be sensibly formulated and asked about the world. Consequently a practically minded person needn't bother with such questions, casting Dostoevsky, Tolstoy, Morrison, and pretty much every religious tradition to the flames.[14]

The most sophisticated branches of legal philosophy were profoundly influenced by this approach, particularly the arguments of Ludwig Wittgenstein and the speech-act theory of John Austin. Most promi-nently H.L.A Hart described law as a union of "primary and secondary rules" whose "core" could be understood by any sufficiently intelligent person familiar with the ordinary meaning of words in her language.[15] This meant that most legal cases could be solved without minimal fuss, muss, or controversy. All Judges were doing in interpreting the law was applying the rule in conformity with the ordinary meaning of the words of a legal text. However, Hart crucially declared that there were, unfor-tunately, "penumbral" cases where there was no settled meaning to a term in ordinary language. In these hard cases, Judges were effectively forced to legislate by relying on their personal beliefs about what the rule should be. Dworkin will later exploit these kinds of difficulties to great effect, by arguing that "penumbral" cases were in fact where our moral disagreements about law sharpen into genuine controversies.

---

[13] Ludwig Wittgenstein. *Philosophical Investigations*, trans. G.E.M Anscombe, P.M.S Hacker, Joachim Schulte. (Oxford, UK: Blackwell Publishing, 2001).

[14] Derek Parfit. *On What Matters: Volume Two*. (Oxford, UK: Oxford University Press, 2011) at pgs 410–411.

[15] See H.L.A Hart. *The Concept of Law: Second Edition*. (Oxford, UK: Oxford Univer-sity Press, 1997) and and H.L.A Hart. "Positivism and the Separation of Law and Morals." *Harvard Law Review*, Vol 71, 1958.

Hart's ordinary language positivism wasn't the only major legal theory to understand the law in largely linguistic terms. Interestingly, while originalists and critical legal theorists usually see themselves as entirely at odds, they often align in the conviction that much of law has to do with language and words. Originalists follow a very crude kind of positivist instinct by insisting that there must be some plain meaning to legal terms, otherwise, Judges would indeed have to assume the role of legislators that Hart figured they inevitably would in hard cases. Where this linguistic idyll lies is a matter of debate. Perhaps it can be found by looking at the intentions of law makers,[16] or maybe in the ordinary dictionary meaning of a legal text at the time it was drafted.[17] But just like heaven, the originalist's faith tells him it is out there somewhere and more real than the shadowy illusions cast by sophisticates; otherwise, he might have to question his moral convictions about what the "neutral" judiciary is doing.

By contrast many critical legal theorists also insisted that the surface of legal dispute is largely about words, but that their meaning is politically contentious the whole way down. Often leaning on a variety of post-modern authors such as Derrida or Foucault, writers like Alan Hutchinson[18] and Stanley Fish pointed out how the plain meaning core of language was hardly benign. It operated as a kind of hegemonic discourse that reified the preferences of the status quo in law and legal interpretation, which "enchanted"[19] legal officials played within by insisting that their pet rethinking of some obscure legal term expressed foundational disagreements about the true meaning of a word. But for these critics, there is no "true" meaning to a word, only a historical discourse about its meaning set by power in the interests of the powerful. Most legal officials attempt to evade this by sublimating power with rhetorical appeals to objectivity, impartiality, and even "science." This ignores that what law will mean is never a question of the final truth

---

[16] Robert Bork. *Coercing Virtue: The Worldwide Rule of Judges.* (Toronto, ON: Vintage Canada, 2002).

[17] Antonin Scalia. *A Matter of Interpretation: Federal Courts and the Law.* (Princeton, NJ: Princeton Paperbacks, 1997).

[18] Allan Hutchinson. *Waiting for C.O.R.A.F.* (Toronto, ON: University of Toronto Press, 1995).

[19] Pierre Schlagg. *The Enchantment of Reason.* (Durham, NC: Duke University Press, 1998).

or falsity of words and their interpretation, but instead a question of who
has power and who does not. Critical legal theorists uniformly took the
side of the subaltern who does not. Though why we should have reason
to morally care about the subaltern if all that can ever be accomplished
is replacing one discourse of power with another remained a riddle crits
struggled to answer.

For Dworkin, legal positivists, originalists, and post-modern critical
legal theorists were all enamored with the same misconceptions about law
and language, which he calls the "semantic sting." Positivists, originalists and others insist there must (usually) be some uncontroversial criteria
for ascertaining the meaning of legal words and then applying them to
empirical contexts. Without such criteria, the whole idea of neutral law
and equally neutral Judges collapses. Critical legal theorists think there
never will be such criteria discovered, and so consequently law is nothing
more than an arbitrary discourse in a hylomorphic relationship to power.
By contrast, for Dworkin any understanding of law inevitably entails a
hermeneutics of interpretation guided by the language of a legal text. But
it is a hermeneutics which brings in an abundance of extra-linguistic material; most importantly the abstract moral principles that underpin basic
legal notions such as *stare decisis*.[20]

> We have drawn the semantic sting and no longer need the caricature of
> legal practices offered in semantic theories. We can see more clearly now,
> and this is what we see. Law is an interpretive concept...Judges normally
> recognize a duty to continue rather than discard a practice they have
> joined. So they develop, in response to their own convictions and instincts,
> working theories about their responsibilities under that practice. When
> they disagree in what I called the theoretical way, their disagreements are
> interpretive. They disagree, in large measure or in fine detail, about the
> soundest interpretation of some pertinent aspect of judicial practice.[21]

For Dworkin, this helps us recognize that debates about interpreting
law aren't really just semantic disputes about the meaning of words;

---

[20] Dworkin argues that stare decisis is held to out of convictions of fairness and equal
treatment.

[21] See Ronald Dworkin. *Law's Empire*. (Cambridge, MA: The Belknap Press of Harvard
University Press, 1986) at pg 87.

they're instead foundational disagreements about the best and most integral way of realizing a moral project. This also has the effect of reinflating moral, political, and legal discourse from the semantic flatness to which it had been relegated by mid-century philosophy. After all debates about what "equality" or "due process" means under the Fourteenth Amendment in *Brown v Board of Topeka* or *Dobbs v Jackson Women's Health Organization* aren't really debates just about what the "meaning" of equality is in a dictionary or in ordinary parlance. Instead, they are truly weighty philosophical disputes about what the best interpretive theory of legal equality is in a society of citizens entitled to equal respect.

KEY DWORKINIAN CONCEPT TWO: THE CRITIQUE OF LEGAL POSITIVISM

When legal positivism emerged as a matter of significant debate. One can trace it back to Thomas Hobbes in the seventeenth century, or if one is feeling especially ambitious even Sextus Empiricus and Han Feizi. But in its modern form legal positivism originated in the writings of Jeremy Bentham and John Austin in the nineteenth century. It quickly evolved into a myriad of different forms. In its Anglicized tradition, legal positivism often aligned with the empirical metaphysics and utilitarian morality ala Bentham through Hart and Joseph Raz. In its continental flavor, various forms of Kantian transcendental idealism and deontology provided a more palatable basis, climaxing in the extraordinarily systematic thinking of Hans Kelsen.

What unites the various flavors of legal positivism together is a commitment to the "separation thesis": that the concept of law and the concept of morality and justice are analytically distinct. This brought early legal positivists into confrontation with the natural law tradition which had been dominant for millennia, and which enjoyed a brief Renaissance in the post-war world. For the legal positivist what law is, what law should be, or even whether one is under an obligation to obey the law are all separate questions. Hart articulates both the history and stakes with admirable clarity in his seminal paper "Positivism and the Separation of Law and Morals":

> At the close of the eighteenth century and the beginning of the nineteenth the most earnest thinkers in England about legal and social problems and the architects of great reforms were the great Utilitarians. Two of them,

Bentham and Austin, constantly insisted on the need to distinguish, firmly and with the maximum of clarity, law as it is from law as it ought to be. This theme haunts their work, and they condemned the natural-law thinkers precisely because they had blurred this apparently simple but vital distinction.[22]

There are many good reasons to embrace legal positivism. One is the fact that, though they differed on a great deal, both Bentham and Kant convincingly locate the source of morality in the human subject and their reason rather than nature. Since morality couldn't be found in nature this meant that the rational morality conceived by human beings may very well conflict with the moral norms embodied in actually existing legal institutions. This had the effect of de-naturalizing existent legal authority and making its legitimacy open to contestation by those who had rational motivations to doubt it. Not coincidentally there was an elective affinity between the most sophisticated exponents of both utilitarian and Kantian legal positivism and a taste for social and legal reform. Secondly, the separation thesis successfully brought a level of analytical clarity to debates by sharpening the distinctions between the concept of law and the concept of morality. At points, this may have been stretched beyond the bounds of plausibility, as Lon Fuller points out when he highlighted how legal positivists tried to translate very moral-sounding norms like *stare decisis* and rights to due process into a more neutral logical or descriptive grammar.[23] But it nevertheless helped overcome the rather ambiguous conflation of natural and man-made law found in the classical tradition. Thirdly, this combination of denaturalization and analytical distinction made it considerably easier to ask questions about whether existent legal systems were in fact just even if they claimed legitimacy for themselves. Most legal positivists understandably resented the Radbruchian complaint that their doctrine had the effect of creating miniature Javerts or Eichmanns who mechanically applied cruel rules on the basis that wicked law still remains law. They pointed out that by stressing how there is no necessary connection between law and morality one can more easily see how a legal system

---

[22] H.L.A Hart. "Positivism and the Separation of Law and Morals." *Harvard Law Review*, Vol 71, 1958 at pg 594.

[23] Lon Fuller. *The Morality of Law: Revised Edition*. (New Haven, CN: Yale University Press, 1969) Lon Fuller. "Positivism and Fidelity to the Law: A Reply to Professor Hart." *Harvard Law Review*, Vol 71, 1958.

may very well be functional while remaining deeply immoral; even to the threshold where one might be under a moral obligation to disobey the law and recognized lawmakers. For Hart at least, this included both the Nazi and apartheid "wicked" legal systems.[24]

Dworkin's objection to positivism centered on Hart's interpretation of law as a union of primary and secondary rules where the criterion for validity is specified by itself a legal rule of recognition.[25] Dworkin described this approach to legality as being a "model of rules." His main line of attack was to foreground how legal officials, most importantly Judges, in fact interpret the law. Dworkin objected that lawyers and Judges don't in fact, and never can even in principle, interpret the law simply as a set of rules whose criteria for application is set by antecedent rules further down the chain till one hits legal bedrock in a rule of recognition or a constitutional grant of lawmaking power; after which one moves from law to discussions of morality and politics. For Dworkin "lawyers reason or dispute about legal rights and obligations, particularly in those hard cases when our problems with these concepts seem most acute, they make use of standards that do not function as rules, but operate differently as principles, policies, and other sorts of standards. Positivism, I shall argue, is a model of and for a system of rules, and its central notion of a single fundamental test for law forces us to miss the important roles of these standards that are not rules."[26] These principles in law may be written down, but they are not exhaustible or capable of being applied in a formalistic way that abnegates a Judge from responsibility for developing a moral and political theory on their best interpretation and application.

The famous case Dworkin gives to express this point in *Hard Cases* and reappears in *Law's Empire* is *Riggs v Palmer* from 1889. In this case, the charming young Elmer Palmer murdered his grandfather Francis Palmer to obtain a substantial inheritance. Caught in the act Elmer was sentenced under criminal law, but still seemed set to inherit his victim's fortune. Francis' children, rather understandably, sued and won. Justice

[24] H.L.A Hart. *The Concept of Law: Second Edition*. (Oxford, UK: Oxford University Press, 1997).

[25] H.L.A Hart. *The Concept of Law: Second Edition*. (Oxford, UK: Oxford University Press, 1997).

[26] Ronald Dworkin. "A Model of Rules." *The University of Chicago Law Review*, Vol 35, 1967 at pg 22.

Robert Earl held that, while there was no strict rule requiring Elmer be disinherited, there were universal maxims of justice which required that one not be allowed to profit from one's crime. In this he prevailed over Judge Gray, who took a more literal reading of the text. Dworkin points out this case, largely uncontroversial, demonstrates how a Judge will rely on different tools to reach a decision-many of them not the rules of the text. This includes looking at the "general principles of law...- judges should construct a statute so as to make it conform as closely as possible to principles of justice assumed elsewhere in the law."[27] For Dworkin it is these principles of justice that for the real heart of law and guide interpretation, especially in hard "penumbral" cases. They can never be formalistically understood as mere rules, text, or intention applied mechanically. Consequently legal positivism cannot stand as a theory of law since the separation thesis and the ideal of strict amoral interpretation—often aligned with rhetoric about Judges being "neutral"—don't hold.

Dworkin's critique of legal positivism is one of the most forceful ever conceived, and it did seem to put the doctrine on the backfoot for a while. Nonetheless, there are important objections one can make; both to defend legal positivism and on more general points. Hart gave a rich reply; objecting that Dworkin's turned on both Judges and the subjects of law taking an "internal" view of the law as legitimate, and consequently respecting efforts to try to interpret law in its best possible light. This ignored that many people take an "external" view of both an individual law and may regard it purely descriptively, as an imposition, or even see the entire legal system as illegitimate.[28] Related to this is the fact that Dworkin often, and especially in *Hard Cases*—the most frequent reference point—emphasizes the standpoint of elite legal officials as determinative of what law is since they are the ones who decide how to make it its best. Many of us who don't think history gives us many good reasons to trust powerful lawyers or judges would argue that the more liberal and indeed democratic approach would be to emphasize how law is conceived by its

---

[27] Ronald Dworkin. *Law's Empire*. (Cambridge, MA: Harvard University Press, 1986) at pg 19.

[28] H.L.A Hart. *The Concept of Law: Second Edition*. (Oxford, UK: Oxford University Press, 1997) at pg 242.

subjects.[29] But Dworkin was broadly correct in arguing that any effort to reduce the interpretation of law down to a formalistic, neutral procedure is bound to fail. Whether one interprets that as a positive, as Dworkin does, or as a sign to be skeptical of juristocracy is another matter.

KEY DWORKINIAN CONCEPT THREE: LAW AS INTEGRITY AND INTERPRETATION

Here, then, is our case for integrity, our reason for striving to see, so far as we can, both its legislative and adjudicative principles vivid in our political life. A community of principle accepts integrity. It condemns checkerboard statutes and less dramatic violations of that ideal as violating the associative character of its deep organization. Internally compromised statutes cannot be seen as flowing from any single coherent scheme of principle; on the contrary, they serve the incompatible aim of a rulebook community, which is to compromise convictions along lines of power. They contradict rather than confirm the commitment necessary to make a large and diverse political society a genuine rather than a bare community: the promise that law will be chosen, changed, developed and interpreted in an overall principles way. A community of principle, faithful to that promise, can claim the authority of a genuine associative community and can therefore claim moral legitimacy-that its collective decisions are matters of obligation and not bare power-in the name of fraternity.[30]

Having rejected the separation thesis and the idea that law is primarily a matter of determining and applying valid rules, Dworkin went on to construct his own wildly ambitious theory of law. This is usually given the shorthand name "law as integrity"; so named after its master principle. In *Law's Empire* Dworkin reintroduces his critique of legal positivism and extends its insights further. Here he directs his primary ire at what Dworkin calls "checkerboard laws" and the form of community they embody and instantiate. The checkerboard conception of laws holds that the legal system consists of a series of discrete cases, policies, statutes, and

---

[29] The legal consciousness literature has made important contributions in this respect. See Patricia Ewick and Susan Silbey. *The Common Place of Law: Stories From Everyday Life.* (Chicago, IL. University of Chicago Press, 1998).

[30] Ronald Dworkin. *Law's Empire.* (Cambridge, MA: Harvard University Press, 1986) at pg 214.

conventions with little intrinsic to do one another. The morass of laws has developed over history in response to the various interests, pressures, and beliefs common at the time and needs to be understood and interpreted pragmatically. As O.W Holmes once put it "the distinctions of the law are founded on experience, not on logic."[31]

Dworkin rejects this checkerboard conception of laws as fundamentally unprincipled at a moral level and also misses an important part of what Judges do when they interpret the law. In a famous thought experiment Dworkin asks us to think about the writing of a chain novel. Each author in the chain from beginning to end is responsible for making the novel the best it can be, and each has his little segment to contribute. This is quite the task, and it will require each author not just to ask what they want the story to be about, but how it will "fit" in with the larger narrative written thus far. Writing a good chain novel will also require them to construct a theory on what the novel is most basically about; a process analogous to asking what the most basic principles of the law will be. One example raised would be asking whether Dicken's *A Christmas Carol* is fundamentally a novel about original sin, the cruelty of Victorian capitalist society and culture, or both![32] In other words, the writers of a chain novels have to be concerned with the level of narrative coherence across the book as a whole. Applying the same kinds of reasoning at the level of principle we call someone who holds consistently to their principles, and whose life consequently coheres in a praiseworthy way, a person of integrity. So too with the laws governing a community.

A community of citizens committed to integrity requires its legal officials to give the best consistent interpretations of the principles underpinning law possible. This by itself would be controversial but Dworkin ups the ante further by saying that this isn't simply a matter of subjective taste or partisan inclination; there is, in fact, one right answer to legal questions as there are to moral and political debates more generally.[33] Though of course Dworkin doesn't deny reaching the right answer may well be difficult; even requiring a superhuman Judge like Justice Hercules

---

[31] O.W Holmes. *The Common Law.* (Cambridge, MA: The Belknap Press of Harvard University Press, 2009) at pgs 281–282.

[32] See Ronald Dworkin "Interview on the Constitution." *Philosophy Overdose,* October 1st 2022, https://www.youtube.com/watch?v=VmjloTrxh1M&t=903s.

[33] Ronald Dworkin. "Objectivity and Truth: You'd Better Believe It." *Philosophy and Public Affairs,* Vol 25, 1996.

to get it right all the time. But a difficult ideal is still a realizable ideal. Moreover Dworkin argues that while a Judge committed to integrity must be sensitive to the "gravitational pull" of precedent, much like a sensitive author in a chain novel has a good sense of the plot thus far, doesn't mean she is chained to it. When a Judge recognizes that present practices simply don't fit with the best interpretation of principles, regardless of past decisions, they may simply disregard precedent as "flotsam and jetsam."[34] In other words, Judges are to be activists when interpreting the law, but not to impose their own political beliefs. Instead, they are active by showing a higher degree of fidelity to the overall integrity of the legal system and its principles than their predecessors.

Dworkin's knock down a practical example on this point is appealing to the seminal *Brown v Board of Education*. Dworkin points out that, after nearly a century of legal precedents such as *Plessy v Ferguson,* it was clear that jurisprudential deference weighed on the side of retaining racist segregation. He also stresses how alternative theories of legal and constitutional interpretation, like intentionalist originalism ala Bork,[35] would clearly have to allow segregation to persist since nowhere did the drafters of the 14th Amendment specify an intention to prohibit segregated institutions. Indeed, many of its drafters explicitly supported them. Consequently, a consistent originalist has to regard, however regrettably, that *Brown* was a legal mistake.[36] But, outside of a few truly committed bigots, even the most pious conservative originalists have balked at rejecting *Brown* since doing so would profoundly discredit the entire approach. By contrast, Dworkin points out how his theory has no problems whatsoever explaining why *Brown* was decided correctly. It represented a more integral interpretation of the principle of equality embedded in the abstract text of the 14th Amendment. Earlier and frankly bad Judges who disagreed with desegregation were simply incorrect in supposing that decisions like *Plessy's* were on the level.

There is undoubtedly something majestic about Dworkin's theory of law as integrity, and as we hope to show it has lost none of its force. Many critics have objected to it. Originalists have fired back that

---

[34] Ronald Dworkin. "Hard Cases." *Harvard Law Review* 88 (1975).

[35] Bork and other originalists insist otherwise, but purely for optical reasons rather than as a matter of theoretical integrity according to Dworkin.

[36] Ronald Dworkin. "Bork's Jurisprudence." *The University of Chicago Law Review,* Vol 57, 1990 at pg 667.

Dworkinian theory is essentially a hyper-intellectualized and sophisti-cated license for left-liberal judges to legislate from the bench while dismissing conservatives as simply being unprincipled. Many undoubt-edly share Judge McConnell's view that Dworkin thinks "judges should simply act as philosophers and impose their moral views in the name of giving meaning to the constitution..."[37] On the other flank a host of post-modern and critical legal objections have raised more serious ques-tions about whether there can genuinely be objectivity in legal analysis; not to mention whether there is in fact much that is genuinely principled and attractive about the left-liberalism of Dworkin's convictions.[38] But excepting Hart-Raz positivism there is no Anglo-American legal theory of comparative philosophical sophistication, sweep and power.

KEY DWORKINIAN CONCEPT FOUR: LIBERAL EGALITARIAN JUSTICE

Beyond just being a seminal legal theorist Dworkin made important contributions to moral and political philosophy from a liberal egalitarian perspective that stands independently. For the most part, they will not be the focus of this book. But it is important to note that Dworkin always regarded his legal theory as part and parcel of a complete account of the unity of value on all levels. In this respect he notably bucked a trend in post-Rawlsian analytical thinking, which largely centered on deflating meta-ethical ambitions and justifying liberal politics and law on more pragmatic or consensual bases. Rawls' *Political Liberalism* or Ely's demo-cratic proceduralism are good examples.[39] By contrast Dworkin's liberal egalitarianism was exceptionally strident and muscular, stressing a unity of principle from beginning to end.

Dworkin explained his approach to liberal egalitarian justice in the opening pages of *Justice for Hedgehogs:*

---

[37] Steven G Calabresi. *Originalism: A Quarter-Century of Debate.* (Washington, DC: Regnery Publishing Inc, 2007) at pg 142.

[38] Pierre Schlag. *The Enchantment of Reason.* (Durham, NC: Duke University Press, 1998).

[39] For Dworkin's critique of these forms of argumentation see Ronald Dworkin. "Rawls and the Law." *Fordham Law Review*, Vol 72, 2004.

The fox knows many things, but the hedgehog knows one big thing. Value is one big thing. The truth about living well and being good and what is wonderful is not only coherent but mutually supporting: what we think about any one of these must stand up, eventually, to any argument we find compelling about the rest. I try to illustrate the unity of at least ethical and moral values: I describe a theory of what living well is like and what, if we want to live well, we must do for, and not do to, other people.[40]

For Dworkin, liberal egalitarian justice is grounded in a particular vision of what it means to live a good life—a life where one is dealt a hand when you are born—your circumstances—and your life is in effect a performance positioned by those circumstances. We make choices in the course of our lives that have consequences, good or bad, and must take personal responsibility for those choices. What distinguishes liberal egalitarian justice for Dworkin is the requirement that government must adopt laws and policies that ensure that its citizens' fates are characterized by equal circumstances—we all should enjoy access to an equal share of resources across our lives.

Such an ambitious view seems audacious, even Icarus-like, in our post-modern age.[41] And indeed it is, and Dworkin recognized that it would be a hard sell in an increasingly skeptical forum. But Dworkin rejected more cynical forms skepticism in whatever form they took post-modern, post-metaphysical, traditionalist conservatism and more. In "Objectivity and Truth: You Better Believe It" he argues that nihilistic "external moral skepticism"—which questions whether there is any value to existence as a whole or whether everything is permitted—is ultimately untenable as a meta-ethical position.[42] This is because no individual could practically hold to it with regard to their own actions, since they would have no reason-giving basis for any moral position they would take-including external skepticism and the view that everything is permitted. In saying

---

[40] Ronald Dworkin. *Justice for Hedgehogs*. (Cambridge, MA. Harvard University Press, 2010) at pg 1.

[41] See Matthew McManus. *The Emergence of Postmodernity at the Intersection of Liberalism, Capitalism, and Secularism*. (Cham, Switzerland: Palgrave MacMillan, 2022).

[42] Interestingly Bernard Williams disagrees, postulating that one might be an entirely consistent nihilistic, but her mode of reasoning would be profoundly constraining and deeply contrary to most recognizably human forms of justification. See Bernard Williams. *Morality: An Introduction to Ethics*. (Cambridge, UK: Cambridge University Press, 2012).

one cannot make meta-ethically compelling statements, one cannot subsequently argue that everything is permitted since that requires committing to a kind of ultra-permissive meta-ethic.[43] The skeptical serpent eats itself and discovers it tastes rotten. By contrast, the far more deadly "internal moral skepticism" forces us to question whether our substantive values are in fact true and not false. One might ask whether liberal values are in fact unjust; nothing more than a license for nihilistic emotivism, class exploitation, decadent materialism, or class and racial oppression. Or one might ask whether it would be better to have never been born or ponder Ivan Karamazov's question of whether even a benevolent God could be forgiven in a world where parents would allow their child to freeze to death in the winter. Against these kinds of skepticism Dworkin argues we can only ever find fortitude by checking our most basic principles and wondering whether they are up to the task of making sense of the meaning of existence.

Dworkin himself was sure that a left-liberalism which held that each individual as worthy of equal respect under the law while entrenching their equal liberty to pursue their vision of what was of highest concern, would be just. This included taking seriously an individual's rights to abortion, assisted suicide, and publishing offensive material. However, equal respect under the law would require a lot more than a state that simply refrained from interfering with one's basic "negative" rights. Most conventional theories of rights are grounded in some sort of libertarian or classical liberal account of the primacy of individual liberty, often leading to conservative positions on issues like gun rights, free speech, taxation, and private property rights. Dworkin sought instead to develop a theory of rights that takes seriously the civil rights movement and other aspects of the counter-majoritarian rights revolution. He famously argued in his first book *Taking Rights Seriously* that rights properly understood are grounded instead in the principle of equal respect and concern and function as trumps on government law and policy when those laws and policies do not treat all citizens as equals.[44]

---

[43] There is a recognizable tinge of Kantian theories of practical reason here, with a significant religious overtone that reminds one of Kierkegaard's claim about the necessity of choice in the face of the absurd.

[44] Ronald Dworkin, Taking *Rights Seriously* (Cambridge, MA: Harvard University Press, 1977), ch. 7.

Much of Dworkin's late work was taken up with a rearguard argument for what he called "equality of resources" modeled on an insurance scheme. Dworkin followed Rawls in arguing that, while each person was responsible for their life, they should not be disadvantaged for reasons that were arbitrary from a moral point of view. He imagined a theoretical scenario where equally endowed shipwrecked individuals on a state-of-nature-like deserted island would distribute resources among themselves through an auction while purchasing insurance against potentially malignant future events like accidents or sickness. What this would look like practically is something Dworkin didn't blueprint out completely. But at various points, he endorsed public insurance, welfare for the poor, access to quality schools for all, and near the end of his life equal value for the political rights of citizens against plutocratic excess.[45]

Key Dworkinian Concept: On Legal Mistakes and Unsettling Post-Liberal Law

In the years since Dworkin died the United States have moved closer to his ideal of liberal justice in some respects. This is particularly—though fragilely—true on issues like LGBTQ rights, which was an early crusade of his.[46] But in most other respects the United States has become a more unjust society. The cruel superficiality of Reaganism has smoothly given way to the outright authoritarianism of Trumpism-a political ideology as lacking in principled integrity as any the modern world has seen. The SCOTUS and the Federal judiciary have moved staunchly to the right on issues ranging from voting rights guarantees to gun control, and most infamously of all on abortion rights. And if the recent *Dobbs* decision is any indicator the fanatics on the Court aren't done yet. In his concurrence with the majority Justice Thomas all but drooled over the illiberal precedent set by *Dobbs,* indicating that "in future cases, we should reconsider all of this Court's substantive due process precedents, including *Griswold,*

---

[45] Ronald Dworkin. "The Decision That Threatens Democracy." *New York Review of Books,* May 13, 2010.

[46] Ronald Dworkin. "Lord Devlin and the Enforcement of Morals" *The Yale Law Journal,* Vol 75, No 6, 1966.

Lawrence, and *Obergefell.*"[47] In the event of another Republican presidency, the Court will doubtless grow even bolder. We'll see a manic effort to SCOTUS longstanding reputation as a bastion of injustice. *Greatest Hits of the US Supreme Court: All Your Faves from Dredd Scott to Bell, including Citizens United and Dobbs.*

This raises the question of what can be done, and how to move on from the injustices of a waxing post-liberal legal paradigm. Here is where Dworkin can be especially insightful. Dworkin continuously insisted on the need for Judges to be attentive to the "gravitational" force of precedent. The reason wasn't just technical but principled; like Lon Fuller, Dworkin recognized that there was a strong moral component to *state decisis.* That is a Judge is committed to a principle of fairness by treating cases alike.[48] But this is qualified by the need to evaluate the arguments of principle necessary to justify those earlier decision; a point that is magnified when a decision is based on deference to the transient policy preference of a given interest group. In circumstances where it becomes obvious that a decision doesn't fit into the "seamless web" of law except as an aberration, a Dworkinian Judge isn't just entitled but required to characterize their judgments as a flat-out "mistake" of principled legal analysis. And since legal analysis must be "forward looking" a Dworkinian Judge like Justice Hercules must be ruthless in recognizing where those mistakes were made. As Dworkin put it in "Hard Cases":

> Hercules must also face a different and greater problem. If the history of his court is at all complex, he will find, in practice, that the requirement of total consistency he has accepted will prove too strong, unless he develops it further to include the idea that he may, in applying this requirement, disregard some part of institutional history as a mistake. For he will be unable, even with his superb imagination, to find any set of principles that reconciles all standing statutes and precedents. This is hardly surprising: the legislators and judges of the past did not all have Hercules' ability or insight, nor were they men and women who were all of the same mind and opinion. Of course, any set of statutes and decisions can be explained historically, or psychologically, or sociologically, but consistency requires justification, not explanation, and the justification must be plausible and

---

[47] See Clarence Thomas, Concurrence in *Dobbs v Jackson Women's Health Organization.* 597_US (2022) at pg 3.

[48] Ronald Dworkin. *Taking Rights Seriously.* (Cambridge, MA: Harvard University Press, 1977) at pg 113.

not sham. If the justification he constructs makes distinctions that are arbitrary and deploys principles that are unappealing, then it cannot count as a justification at all.[49]

In circumstances where a clear mistake, or even a long history of mistakes has been made Dworkin holds out several possible remedies. He stresses that Judges must not make "impudent" use of their power to hold that a large series of legal decisions were mistaken. In some circumstances, a Dworkinian Judge will allow a decision to stand, but simply limit its gravitational force for future decisions; in effect neutering its status as a precedent. But in more serious cases it may come to the fore that some previous decision, enthusiastically accepted at the time, is now widely regarded as deeply unjust given the conceptions of fairness present within the community. A "particular principle, though it once had sufficient appeal to persuade a legislature or court to a legal decision, has now so little force that it is unlikely to generate any further such decisions, then the argument from fairness that supports that principle is undercut. If he can show by arguments of political morality that such a principle, apart from its popularity, is unjust, then the argument from fairness that supports that principle is overridden."[50] In these circumstances, the gravitational force of a mistaken decision is so diluted it cannot survive the loss and must be completely overturned.

Seen from this standpoint the recent SCOTUS decisions look like a pugnacious chain of all but willful "mistakes." This is because, as we will explore in the remainder of this book, there are no good principled reasons for eroding liberal democratic protections for the least well off in the American community. The SCOTUS' post-liberal decisions demonstrably lack persuasive force for the community—indeed many are deeply unpopular—and do not convince as arguments from political morality. Indeed in many cases, the post-liberal Court's reasoning "cannot count as a justification at all" for its decisions if the aspiration is truly to make the American constitutional order the best it can be through a firm commitment to the integrity of its principles. Given this, a paradigm shift in legal thinking is required which will treat the precedents set by post-liberal law as so much flotsam and jetsam to be rejected by more resolutely principled future jurists.

---

[49] Ronald Dworkin. "Hard Cases." *Harvard Law Review* 88 (1975) at pg 1097.

[50] Ronald Dworkin. "Hard Cases." *Harvard Law Review* 88 (1975) at pg 1101.

CHAPTER 3

Securing Constitutional Democracy

Abstract This chapter engages Dworkin's pioneering concept of democracy as a kind of "partnership" that requires the law to show equal respect and concern to citizens. It then applies Dworkinean principles to evaluating his seminal critique of the *Citizens United* decision, demonstrating why and how it threatens democracy. This chapter also discusses some of the limitations of Dworkinean democracy, particularly with regard to the workplace.

Keyword Partnership democracy · Majoritarian democracy · *Citizens united* · Workplace democratization

Liberalism and Democracy: Articles of Conciliation

No nation's politics can be run like a philosophy seminar; a democracy must give the final verdict on who leads it to many millions of people who have no training in economics, philosophy, foreign policy, or environmental science and who do not have the time or perhaps the ability to achieve much competence in these disciplines. But our national politics fails the

L. A. Jacobs and M. McManus, *Against Post-Liberal Courts and Justice*, Palgrave Studies in Classical Liberalism, https://doi.org/10.1007/978-3-031-45347-2_3

standards of even a decent junior high school debate. Our candidates much us squirm with embarrassment when they clear their throats to speak. They are ruled by consultants who tell them that style is everything and content nothing, tat they must say as little as possible except in subliminal codes meant secretly to energize important groups, that a punchy sound bite on the evening news is political gold, and anything remotely resembling an actual argument is death.[1]

Ronald Dworkin, Is Democracy Possible Here?

Liberalism's (bad) friends[2] and enemies[3] alike have long insisted that there are no necessary conceptual, or even particularly good historical, links between liberalism and democracy. While the two have become practically synonymous in the public lexicon, such that the term "liberal democracy" is taken to be coextensive with the democratic project, many other systems of government past and present have claimed the title.[4] Plenty of liberals have historically shared James Madison's deep reservations that a "pure" democracies have "ever been spectacles of turbulence and contention; have every been found incompatible with personal security or the rights of property; and have in general been as short in their lives as they have been violent in their deaths."[5] Perhaps unsurprisingly for a state founded by such men—not to mention men so lovingly attached to property they become flustered at the mere thought of it being compromised—it is even hard to argue that the American constitution is particularly democratic. As Dahl points out, while innovative by eighteenth century standards, by now ol' "bundle of compromises" falls "far short of the requirements that later generations would find necessary and desirable in a democratic republic."[6]

---

[1] See Ronald Dworkin. *Is Democracy Possible Here: Principles for a New Political Debate.* (Princeton, NJ: Princeton University Press, 2006) at pgs 127–128.

[2] See F.A Hayek. *Law, Legislation and Liberty.* (Chicago, IL: University of Chicago Press, 2022).

[3] See Carl Schmitt. Constitutional Theory, trans. Jeffrey Seitzer. (Durham, NC. Duke University Press, 2008).

[4] See Robert Dahl. *On Democracy.* (New Haven, CN: Yale University Press, 2000).

[5] See Alexander Hamilton, James Madison, John Jay. *The Federalist Papers.* (New York, NY: Signet, 2003) at pg 76.

[6] See Robert Dahl. *How Democratic is the American Constitution.* (New Haven, CN: Yale University Press, 2003) at pg 15.

For many of us, this democratic inadequacy constitutes a serious mark against both liberalism and the constitution of a country ever aspiring to be the "world's greatest democracy." And yet even progressive critics of democracy have—at times begrudgingly—admitted that liberals are correct to express reservations about pure majoritarianism and its potential for tyranny.[7] After all, while for an egalitarian Madison was wrong to resist the capacity of democratic majorities to redistribute the wealth of elites, he was no doubt right to be worried about the persecution of far less well-heeled minorities. Indeed, as contemporary critics of democracy continue to remind us, there are few things more potentially illiberal tyrannical than a majority who regards its bigoted opinions as license precisely because they have been chosen by the majority in its own interests.[8] These are not merely hypothetical concerns either; many post-liberal and nationalist intellectuals explicitly committed to rejecting human equality see exclusionary forms of populist "illiberal" or "conservative" democracy as an attractive form of government.[9]

Unfortunately in responding to the prospects of illiberal democracy, many liberals (and libertarians) have given into their most elitist impulses; calling for the establishment of "epistocracy" or even demanding that the "elites" rise up against the "ignorant" masses.[10] This is entirely the wrong response to a context where a major basis for the animosity to liberalism is the sense that the liberal state is unresponsive, dominated by elites, and increasingly corrupted by the influence of money.[11] In such a context we need a democratic theory that is sensitive to the need to protect liberal freedom, while at the same time offering the conceptual resources to articulate demands for more robust forms of social or republican freedom through securing equal value for the political liberties of citizens.

---

[7] See Irving Howe. "Liberalism and Socialism: Articles of Conciliation?" *Dissent Magazine*, Winter, 1977.

[8] See Jason Brennan. *Against Democracy*. (Princeton, NJ: Princeton University Press, 2016).

[9] See Yoram Hazony. "Conservative Democracy: Liberal Principles Have Brought Us a Dead End." First Things, January 2019.

[10] See Jason Brennan. *Against Democracy*. (Princeton, NJ: Princeton University Press, 2016) and James Traub. "It's Time For the Elites to Rise Up Against the Ignorant Masses." *Foreign Policy*, June 28th, 2016.

[11] See Roger Eatwell and Matthew Goodwin. *National Populism: The Revolt Against Liberal Democracy*. (London, UK: Penguin Books, 2018).

Dworkin's theory of democracy offers many such resources, though this must be qualified. Dworkin is a liberal and a democratic theorist, but certainly not a majoritarian. The relationship between liberalism and democracy is not always a comfortable one for him, whether in theory or practice. In an American context where two controversial recent Presidential nominees were elected after losing the popular vote, Dworkin's reservations about majoritarian legitimacy might strike many egalitarians as uncouth. More importantly, his never boundless always faithful defense of American judges and judicial review, have been subject to important critiques.[12] Indeed, given the shameful record of the SCOTUS on issues relating to democratic equality and citizenship—especially when race enters the picture[13]—there are many respects in which Dworkin's faith in Courts can appear borderline naive in terms of its practical politics. But as a matter of principle Dworkin's argument that democracy must entail more than mere majoritarian rule remains deeply inspiring. The question therefore becomes whether it can be resuscitated in light of its practical limitations.

THE PARTNERSHIP VIEW OF DEMOCRACY

Is Democracy Possible Here? constitutes Dworkin's most mature and sustained treatment discussion of the state of the union. Written during the darkest days of the Bush Administration's war on terror, and shortly before the 2008 recession plunged neoliberal capitalism into a near-crisis of existential legitimacy, the book is notable for Dworkin's uncharacteristically pessimistic tone. The book opens with the claim that, much as in 2023, "American politics are in an appalling state" where people "disagree, fiercely, about almost everything."[14] This corrosive partisanship has undermined citizens' capacity to disagree with one another through

---

[12] See Pierre Schlag. "The Empty Circles of Liberal Justification." Michigan Law Review 96 (1997) and Pierre Schlag. The Enchantment of Reason. (Durham, NC: Duke University Press, 1998).

[13] See Dred Scott v. Sandford, 60 U.S. 393 (1856), Plessy v. Ferguson, 163 U.S. 537 (1896), Williams v. Mississippi, 170 U.S. 213 (1898) and more recently Citizens United vs Federal Electoral Committee (2010) Shelby County v. Holder, 570 U.S. 529 (2013and Brnovich v. Democratic National Committee, 594 U.S. (2021).

[14] See Ronald Dworkin. *Is Democracy Possible Here: Principles for a New Political Debate.* (Princeton, NJ: Princeton University Press, 2006) at pg 1.

argumentation and has reduced democratic politics to a winner-take-all all Schmittian contest between theologically opposed enemies.[15] In such a contest between "red" and "blue" states whoever happens to obtain power by winning slightly more (or in Bush's case, slightly less) of the country's support at any given time sees uses it as an opportunity to unilaterally ram through policies which appeal to their base while marginalizing the opposition as much as possible.

For Dworkin, the crisis resulted from a rejection of the best impulses of democracy and an embrace of the worst. Far from a union of equal citizens, America was once more a house divided against itself. Rather than regarding Americans who disagreed with one's political views as fellow citizens who warranted respect, instead, they were so many "libtards" or "deplorables" corrupted the whole way down. Instead of trying to persuade the opposition or the undecided, vast and growing sums of money were spent trying to mobilize the base and silence dissent. And unfortunately, things have only grown worse since 2006. From Mitt Romney's patrician announcement that "47%" of Americans were too dependent on government to support him, to Obama and Clintons' smug dismissal of "deplorables" who "cling to guns or religion or antipathy toward people wo aren't like them," things climaxed with Trump venomously describing Democrats as "treasonous" "un-American" and "enemies of the people." Things are a long way from Pericles' romance of a democratic society where "we are not suspicious of one another, nor angry with our neighbor if he does what he likes; we do not put on sour looks at him which, though harmless, are not pleasant."

Dworkin insists that to get things back on track we need to reject a "view" of democracy as purely majoritarian, according to which "democracy is government by majority will, that is, in accordance with the will of the greatest number of people, expressed in elections with universal or near universal suffrage." In a majoritarian democracy there is "no guarantee that a majority will decide fairly; its decisions may be unfair to minorities whose interests the majority systematically ignores."[16] It is

---

[15] See Carl Schmitt. The Concept of the Political: Expanded Edition. (Chicago, IL. The University of Chicago Press, 2007) and Adrian Vermuele. "All Human Conflict is Ultimately Theological." Church Life Journal, July 26th, 2019.

[16] See Ronald Dworkin. *Is Democracy Possible Here: Principles for a New Political Debate.* (Princeton, NJ: Princeton University Press, 2006) at pg 131.

also the case that there is nothing in the concept of majoritarian democracy that requires justificatory argumentation about policy or principle to be particularly good. "After all" the people "are not crying out for more sophisticated political argument; they are busy, they do not mind being entertained, and the great majority of them know what they think anyway."[17] Moreover, while on the surface a purely majoritarian democracy might appear deeply egalitarian on the basis that the principle of one person one vote would seem to equalize political power, Dworkin insists that this is not actually the case. This is because, absent a grant of non-fungible rights which inhibit the exercise of domination against minorities and vulnerable populations, it is very possible for a tyrannical majority and/or their representatives to hemorrhage unequal and oppressive power into their hands.[18] This in turn raises the partisan stakes of majoritarian democracy because those who don't win an election would have little legal capacity to resist domination by a majority and its representatives, which incentivizes doing anything one can to win and dreading the prospect of losing.[19]

Of course, Dworkin doesn't reject majority decision making in many contexts, since after a certain threshold this would simply entail removing one's self from the democratic universe entirely. He is making the more modest theoretical and historical claim "United Sates is a more just society than it would have been had its constitutional rights been left to the conscience of majoritarian institutions."[20] Instead Dworkin argues we need a "deeper and more elaborate account that tells us what conditions must be met and protected in a political community before majority rule

---

[17] See Ronald Dworkin. *Is Democracy Possible Here: Principles for a New Political Debate.* (Princeton, NJ: Princeton University Press, 2006) at pg 132.

[18] See Ronald Dworkin. *Is Democracy Possible Here: Principles for a New Political Debate.* (Princeton, NJ: Princeton University Press, 2006) at pgs 141–143.

[19] We've drawn in part on the republican or "Neo-Roman" language of non-domination here since it helps clarify the parameters of the discussion. Dworkin himself rarely uses it, and there are debates about the overlap between republican freedom and liberalism, but there is some license to do so. Commentators have increasingly pointed out how many of the political liberties cherished by liberals can be better articulated through a republican language than that of, say, negative freedom. See Hannah Dawson and Annelien de Dijn. *Rethinking Liberty Before Liberalism.* (Cambridge, UK: Cambridge University Press, 2023).

[20] See Ronald Dworkin. *Law's Empire.* (Cambridge, MA: Harvard University Press, 1986) at pg 356.

is appropriate for that community."[21] This "deeper and more elaborate" account aligns with what Dworkin calls the "partnership" view of democracy predicated on two principles: the government must show equal concern to all citizens and that citizens or "the people" are entitled to self-government.[22] These directly correspond to still deeper Dworkinean commitment to human dignity about the equal and intrinsic value of all human life, and the fact that each individual has a unique responsibility and freedom for living a successful life. As Dworkin puts it:

> According to the...partnership view of democracy however, democracy means that the people govern themselves each as a full partner in a collective political enterprise so that a majority's decisions are democratic only when certain further conditions are met that protect the status and interests of each citizen as a full partner in that enterprise. On the partnership view, a community that steadily ignores the interests of some minority or other group is just for that reason not democratic even though it elects its officials by impeccably majoritarian means.[23]

Now there are respects in which Dworkin's "partnership view" of democracy may appear somewhat constrained to modern readers. For one, it adopts the familiar liberal approach of conceiving democracy purely in statist terms and extending principled analysis to state institutions. It has very little to say about what Elizabeth Anderson rightly calls the despotism entailed by "private government."[24] Given that most of us will spend much (maybe even a majority) of our waking life working for an employer, it is not clear why these should not be more equal partnerships where workers' human value is better appreciated. Dworkin's failure to extend the egalitarian principles of democratic partnership to the workplace likely results from his rather narrow conception[25] of

[21] See Ronald Dworkin. *Is Democracy Possible Here: Principles for a New Political Debate.* (Princeton, NJ: Princeton University Press, 2006) at pg 143.

[22] See Ronald Dworkin. *Is Democracy Possible Here: Principles for a New Political Debate.* (Princeton, NJ: Princeton University Press, 2006) at pgs 144–145.

[23] See Ronald Dworkin. *Is Democracy Possible Here: Principles for a New Political Debate.* (Princeton, NJ: Princeton University Press, 2006) at pg 131.

[24] See Elizabeth Anderson. *Private Government: How Employers Rule Our Lives (And Why We Don't Talk About It).* (Princeton, NJ: Princeton University Press, 2017).

[25] The same cannot be said of Dworkin'scounterpart Rawls, who in his last work became more sensitive to the importance of the Marxist and socialist traditions and their

the Marxist and more generally socialist traditions.[26] Mirroring his liberal democratic focus on the state he seems to understand socialism in purely statist and collectivist terms, ignoring the tradition's important critiques of workplace domination.[27] This would also enrich his analysis of the disparities in democratic power which result from inequities of wealth and economic status; a matter of impassioned concern later in Dworkin's life. For instance, even in his seminal analysis of the influence of money on American democracy circa a critique of the *Citizens United* decision, Dworkin has little to say about where countervailing centers of democratic power might emerge which would secure the more equal value of political liberties for all citizens. Reconstructing the labor and trade union movements decimated by neoliberal reforms would be a valuable place to start.

Nevertheless, as a principled ideal, there is much about the "partnership" view of democracy that can commend itself to liberals specifically and egalitarians more generally. Dworkin is undoubtedly right that a purely majoritarian democracy provides few intrinsic safeguards against the accumulation of highly unequal power in the hands of majorities and their representatives, who will all too often be swayed by prejudice and fear. More admirably still, Dworkin innovates by refusing to channel these concerns into the transparently elitist politics of Madison or Hayek, who often write as though it may be necessary to trade off deep moral commitments to equality to secure liberal freedom and rights. Instead Dworkin makes the important point that for a state to truly respecting the equal intrinsic value of human life by showing equal concern to its citizens, it must secure rights for all against varied forms of domination, including majoritarian domination. This includes securing equal value for political liberties as perhaps the most vital step for a partnership democracy.

---

compatibility with political liberalism and justice as fairness. See John Rawls. Justice as Fairness: A Restatement. (Cambridge, MA. The Belknap Press of Harvard University Press, 2001). Also see William A. Edmundson. John Rawls: Reticent Socialist. (Cambridge, UK: Cambridge University Press, 2017).

[26] This point was raised by Moyn in a very sharp critique of liberal egalitarianism more generally. See Samuel Moyn. Not Enough: Human Rights in an Unequal World. (Cambridge, MA: Belknap Press of Harvard University Press, 2019).

[27] Ronald Dworkin. *Is Democracy Possible Here?: Principles for a New Political Debate.* (Princeton, NJ: Princeton University Press, 2006) at pgs 105–106.

SECURING A PARTNERSHIP DEMOCRACY
PART I: AGAINST *CITIZENS UNITED*

One of Dworkin's greatest works came late in life and was, in terms of its scale, rather minor and unassuming. It was his seminal critique of the *Citizens United* decision in the *New York Review of Books*. Not coincidentally, it is also where Dworkin finally expresses reservations about the potential of courts to enact the kind of liberal egalitarian vision he wanted for the United States. In the next two sections, we will discuss both of these developments through an analysis of both the initial decision and Dworkin's response to it. This can help us put meatier flesh on the bones of Dworkinean partnership democracy, which even he characterized as something of a "rough sketch."[28]

   Citizens United is a quintessentially American case; involving Hilary Clinton, conservatives angry at Hilary Clinton, and a sweeping decision that the best way to please everyone must be to let the almighty dollar speak. It began in 2002 with the passage of the *Bipartisan Campaign Reform Act*, conceived and pushed by Senator John McCain of the Republican Party and Senator Russ Feingold of the Democrats. The *Reform Act* prevented corporations and unions from spending money electioneer from within 30 days of a primary and 60 days of an election. Several years later, inspired by liberal filmmaker Michael Moore's unprecedented financial success with the anti-Bush polemic *Fahrenheit 9/11*, the conservative non-profit organization Citizens United produced *Hilary: The Movie*. This film was highly critical of then Senator Hilary Clinton, who at that time was running a primary contest against future President Barack Obama. Citizens United wanted to air advertisements for their film during the electoral cycle but were prevented from doing so by the *Reform Act*. Citizens United pursued litigation, and by 2009 the matter was before the Supreme Court. In point of fact, the decision exclusively concerned whether Citizens United was entitled to air *Hilary: The Movie* during the periods prohibited by the *Act*. If the Court had simply granted them permission it might have increased the level of hot air in an already ecologically partisan environment, but the case would likely have disappeared. Instead, in a staggeringly expansive decision the Court decided

---

[28] See Ronald Dworkin. *Is Democracy Possible Here?: Principles for a New Political Debate.* (Princeton, NJ: Princeton University Press, 2006) at pg 145.

to simply do away with all limits on the money corporations-themselves nothing more than legal fictions-could spend on electioneering.

The majority 5/4 opinion was written by Justice Kennedy, with concurrences from Scalia, Thomas, and Roberts. Briefly, they held that the *Reform Act* imposed undue restrictions on speech in violation of the First Amendment. This applied not only to individual citizens but also associations of individuals like corporations. The majority then went further and held that since spending money is vital to disseminating speech, restrictions on expenditure also violate the protections guaranteed by the First Amendment. While many would regard cherishing the speech of legal fiction and wanting to help them disseminate their views as more than a little odd, in fact according to Justice Kennedy it is precisely because these legal fictions dominate so much of the economy that we should wish to further amplify their voice.

> The censorship we now confront is vast in its reach. The Government has "muffle[d] the voices that best represent the most significant segments of the economy." McConnell, supra, at 257–258 (opinion of SCALIA, J.). And "the electorate [has been] deprived of information, knowledge and opinion vital to its function." CIO, 335 U. S., at 144 (Rutledge, J., concurring in result). By suppressing the speech of manifold corporations, both for-profit and non-profit, the Government prevents their voices and viewpoints from reaching the public and advising voters on which persons or entities are hostile to their interests. Factions will necessarily form in our Republic, but the remedy of "destroying the liberty" of some factions is "worse than the disease." The Federalist No. 10, p. 130 (B. Wright ed. 1961) (J. Madison). Factions should be checked by permitting them all to speak, see ibid., and by entrusting the people to judge what is true and what is false.[29]

Kennedy then goes on to stress how there is something deeply unfair about this "censorship" since corporations can still lobby the government, and very wealthy individuals could use limitless amounts of money to express themselves. Rather than seeing this as cause for concern, Kennedy laments that "wealthy corporations could still lobby elected officials, although smaller corporations may not have the resources to do so. And wealthy individuals and unincorporated associations can spend

---

[29] See *Citizens United v Federal Election Commission*, No. 08–205, 558 U.S. 310 (2010) at pg 38.

unlimited amounts on independent expenditures...Yet certain disfavored associations of citizens—those that have taken on the corporate form—are penalized for engaging in the same political speech."[30] Kennedy acknowledges that these expenditures may have a corrupting influence on politics and suggests that the legislature may take some steps in light with the constitution to fix them. But this cannot include putting limitations on expenditures, since there cannot be such a thing as too much speech. Or in this case too much license to amplify the volume of the rich's speech from a shrill drone to a Wagnerian tumult.

Justice Stevens no doubt captured the bafflement of many when he observed that ""while American democracy is imperfect, few outside the majority of this Court would have thought its faults included a dearth of corporate money in politics."[31] Dworkin himself was even more cutting. In one of his most charged observations as a legal analyst, he opens "The Decision That Threatens Democracy" with the observation that "...the five conservative justices, on their own initiative, at the request of no party to the suit, declared that corporations and unions have a constitutional right to spend as much as they wish on television election commercials specifically supporting or targeting particular candidates."[32] What followed was one of his most withering critiques finding its ideal target.

Dworkin began by stressing that since the passage of the *Tilman Act* in 1907 there were over 100 years of precedents regarding corporations, which are legal fictions, as not possessing the same First Amendment rights as people. This had been affirmed a mere 20 years before in *Austin v Michigan Chamber of Commerce* decision. Of course we've already seen how, for Dworkin, the existence of a precedent is not itself determinative of the right answer in a hard case. But it does indicate how inconsistent the Court's decision was, and as we'll see, this inconsistency relates back to the fundamental principles of the constitution determinative of law's integrity. Indeed, as Dworkin pointed out this wasn't even a particularly

---

[30] See *Citizens United v Federal Election Commission*, No. 08–205, 558 U.S. 310 (2010) at pg 40.

[31] See *Citizens United v Federal Election Commission*, No. 08–205, 558 U.S. 310 (2010) at pg 90.

[32] See Ronald Dworkin. "The Decision that Threatens Democracy." The New York Review of Books, May 13, 2010.

partisan point. Surveying the various theories applied to principled interpretation of the First Amendment, he points out that "absolutely none of
them—justifies the damage the five conservative justices have just inflicted
on our politics."[33]

Warming his argument up, Dworkin begins by taking aim at the
empirical assertion that allowing corporations the right to spend money
electioneering is consistent with producing an "informed electorate."
This is one of the major theoretical claims which has historically guided
interpretations of the First Amendment and was rhetorically leaned on
very heavily by Justice Kennedy in his decision. Dworkin points out
that that Kennedy offered no compelling reasons "for supposing that
allowing rich corporations to swamp elections with money will in fact
produce a better-informed public—and there are many reasons to think it
will produce a worse-informed one. Corporations have no ideas of their
own. Their ads will promote the opinions of their managers, who could
publish or broadcast those opinions on their own or with others of like
mind through political action committees (PACs) or other organizations
financed through voluntary individual contributions." Indeed corporate
political advertising may well mislead the public because "its volume will
suggest more public support than there actually is for the opinions the
ads express."

But the more important argument for Dworkin is that allowing for
corporations to spend money to electioneer will undermine the public's
political education by monopolizing expressive power in the hands of
wealthy firms. Dworkin rightly points out that, like monopolies elsewhere,
tremendous concentrations of expressive power generate market distor-
tions by not allowing for fair competition of ideas. It would allow monied
parties to sway public opinion more effectively in their interests while
crowding out alternative political viewpoints.

Moving on, Dworkin acknowledges that one might object that this is
the price that has to be paid to respect the dignity and equal status of our
corporate partners, who deserve as much of a chance as anyone to have
their say in democracy. Kennedy appealed to this kind of reasoning when
he claimed that "…by taking the right to speak from some and giving it
to others the Government deprives the disadvantaged person or class of
the right to use speech to strive to establish worth, standing, and respect

---

[33] See Ronald Dworkin. "The Decision that Threatens Democracy." *The New York
Review of Books*, May 13, 2010.

for the speaker's voice."[34] But as Dworkin points out this cannot apply to corporations, who are not individuals and consequently lack dignity and moral interests. Were Kennedy to extend his reasoning a bit further it might seem unjust to not grant corporations the right to vote since that would be depriving them of a basic entitlement granted to others (Dworkin pulled a risky move here in giving a bad court worse ideas).

Finally Dworkin stresses how allowing corporations the power to electioneer will inevitably corrupt elections since it will influence the behavior and decisions of candidates and politicians running for office who might be tempted or threatened by corporate bodies. While Kennedy denied that this was possible so long as corporations don't directly "coordinate" with candidates, Dworkin rightly stressed that it was "naïve" to suppose that candidates and politicians running for office would be "unaware of or indifferent to the likelihood of a heavily financed advertising campaign urging voters to vote for him, if he worked in a corporation's interests, or against him if he did not. No coordination—no role of any candidate or his agents in the design of the ads—would be necessary."[35]

Throughout "The Decision That Threatens Democracy" Dworkin's tone is focused and even unusually polemical, as when he concludes with the ominous observation the "Supreme Court's conservative phalanx has demonstrated once again its power and will to reverse America's drive to greater equality and more genuine democracy. It threatens a step-by-step return to a constitutional stone age of right-wing ideology."[36] This means that the essay for the most part avoids the more measured and highly abstract principled issues engaged in defending a "partnership" democracy. For these reasons, and perhaps to avoid belaboring the polemic with needless baggage, Dworkin avoids directly linking his critique of the decision with the broader political and moral project. But it isn't hard to align the two. While Dworkin denied that citizens need to possess fully equal capacities to influence political decisions, the wildly distorting inequities emerging from a decision like *Citizens United* undoubtedly pushes things too far. Indeed, it progresses from a partnership model of

[34] See Ronald Dworkin. "The Decision that Threatens Democracy." *The New York Review of Books*, May 13, 2010.

[35] Ronald Dworkin. "The Decision that Threatens Democracy." *The New York Review of Books*, May 13, 2010.

[36] Ronald Dworkin. "The Decision that Threatens Democracy." *The New York Review of Books*, May 13, 2010.

democracy of the sort Dworkin argued for and moves directly towards the kind of neoliberal model of democratic rule where every citizen (and every corporation) can vote with their dollar (if they have a dollar). But a majority have a few hundred votes at most, while the minuscule elite who govern corporations and own the means of production gain yet another "immensely powerful weapon" to lobby for causes that benefit them. Very potentially at the expense of most citizens' preferences.[37] This is not a partnership democracy, but closer to a managed and plutocratic polyarchy.[38]

SECURING A PARTNERSHIP DEMOCRACY PART II: THE EQUAL VALUE OF POLITICAL LIBERTIES

Dworkin's critique of *Citizens United* is a powerful one because the ideal of partnership democracy is a powerful one; particularly in our era of radically deepening inequality.[39] Above all else Dworkin demonstrates how one can elegantly develop a powerful democratic theory that retains important anti-majoritarian safeguards without succumbing to anti-egalitarianism. Indeed what is important about partnership democracy is precisely that it demonstrates why and how equality entails far more than just majority rule if it is to be genuinely grounded in equal respect for all citizens. Nevertheless, there are problems with Dworkin's arguments which require consideration.

The first is that, while Dworkin eventually came to view the Supreme Court as a revanchist institution warding off "greater equality and more genuine democracy," he never adequately revised his muscular endorsement of judicial review in light of these changing circumstances. This was perhaps inevitable. Dworkin's judicial theory was deeply entwined with faith that powerful Judges like Hercules would advance law as integrity, and that this is not only consistent but complementary to Dworkin's political theory endorsing partnership democracy. Where powerful

---

[37] See Ronald Dworkin. "The Decision that Threatens Democracy." *The New York Review of Books*, May 13, 2010 and Martin Gilens and Benjamin I Page. "Testing Theories of American Politics: Elites, Interests Groups, and Average Citizens." *Perspectives on Politics*, Vol 12, 2014.

[38] See Robert Dahl. *On Democracy*. (New Haven, CN: Yale University Press, 2000).

[39] See Thomas Piketty. *Capital and Ideology*, trans. Arthur Goldhammer. (Cambridge, MA: Harvard University Press, 2020).

Judges choose to reject the law as integrity and advance political opinions contrary to partnership democracy, Dworkin's tactic was to accuse them of making the wrong legal decision and (more indirectly) failing to advance the ideal political theory. But it is deeply unclear why fundamentally elitist figures like Judges, particularly in a country with a deeply politicized judicial system dominated by conservatives as in the United States, would be interested in advancing either law as integrity or partnership democracy. Granted the power to make sweeping decisions, and unaccountable to the electoral system, it is no surprise that SCOTUS would slip into its long-standing history of making elitist and anti-democratic rulings. As Samuel Moyn reminds us:

> When the U.S. Constitution first became attractive in the late nineteenth century, it was among conservatives facing the frightening prospect of mass suffrage and finding in James Madison's handiwork a device for potentially weathering the coming tempest. Englishman Sir Henry James Sumner Maine, to take one example, sang the praises of the U.S. Constitution as "the most important political instrument of modern times" in his Popular Government (1885), for it "proved" the existence of "several expedients" that would allow the "difficulties" besetting any country "transforming itself" into a democracy to be "greatly mitigated" or "altogether overcome." Unsurprisingly, the powers of the U.S. Supreme Court ranked high on the list of such "expedients." American constitutional practice in this era reflected these antidemocratic virtues. American conservatives retrieved from obscurity the case of Marbury v. Madison (1803), which according to myth proclaimed the power of judicial review of legislation under the Constitution (though in reality it did no such thing). Judges suddenly began invalidating more statutes, throwing out progressive legislation at both federal and state levels. It took the strife of the Great Depression, and fear of Franklin Roosevelt, to cow the institution into getting with the progressive program.[40]

Given this long-standing history Dworkin's rhetorical suggestion that decisions like *Citizens United* constitute a profound break from the Court's long-standing role as a friend of equality and democracy look almost as naïve as Justice Kennedy's conviction that corporate money would never, ever directly influence the decisions of politicians. But this shouldn't lead progressives to the conclusion that law as integrity or

---

[40] See Samuel Moyn. "The Court is Not Your Friend." *Dissent Magazine*, Winter 2020.

partnership democracy are intrinsically flawed, let alone that the solution should be turning to majoritarian democracy. Instead, a fleshed-out Dworkinian theory of partnership democracy complemented by judicial review needs to take seriously the importance of democratizing the judicial system itself. Especially important will be diversifying the backgrounds of the kinds of students who go onto law school by making it more economically accessible. Aligned with this should be a more concerted effort to redirect attention away from prestige schools defined by legacy appointments and often attracting the most affluent students. Access to justice needs to be made more affordable, and programs should be set up that make it easier for the disadvantaged to begin suits and more prestigious and lucrative for talented jurists to take on their causes.[41] Finally, mirroring the efforts of conservative activists in the "law and economics movement" to shift judicial thinking in a right wing direction, legal education should be more socially and empirically oriented.[42] This would draw attention to the profound structural inequities engendered by law in our society, demonstrating how far from a "partnership" between equal citizens we truly are. Were these steps taken it would be quite possible to foster a judiciary that is more receptive to advancing partnership democracy and less fetishistically attached to reified ideas of corporate personhood and plutocracy.

Equally importantly, Dworkin's blanket insistence that "equal political power is a myth" and "not even an attractive myth because we would not want a Martin Luther King Jr. to have only the political influence that you and I do" needs to be scrutinized closely.[43] Here we see Dworkin conflate power and influence in a way that seems not only conceptually odd, but unappealing from the standpoint of partnership democracy. It is undoubtedly true that strict equality of political influence is unobtainable, not necessarily desirable, and not even desired by all. Many would undoubtedly be content as "Hobbits" having little influence on the outside world

---

[41] See Hazel Genn, Paths to Justice: What People Do and Think about Going to Law, (Oxford, UK: Hart Publishing, 1999).

[42] In itself this is a fascinating story. See Steven Teles. *The Rise of the Conservative Legal Movement: The Battle for Control of the Law.* (Princeton, NJ: Princeton University Press, 2010).

[43] See Ronald Dworkin. *Is Democracy Possible Here?: Principles for a New Political Debate.* (Princeton, NJ: Princeton University Press, 2006) at pg 142.

so long as it has little influence on them.[44] But as the republican tradition has taught us, there is a meaningful difference between consciously reneging on influencing the outside world, or even being unable to influence others effectively, and being dominated through the persistence of unequal power. This difference is not cut and dry, since as Foucault has taught us discursive influence very quickly crystallizes into power and vice versa.[45] But from the political standpoint of a democratic theory committed to equal respect for citizens, it is reasonable to argue that the law should try to establish a relative parity of power where possible. This would, in turn, contribute to a fairer exercise of influence since being able to transform influence into political power would depend on dialogical persuasion within the public sphere. Finally, it would inhibit the colonization of the "lifeworld" of citizens where public reason is deliberated by the "system" of power, including economic power of the sort Dworkin expressed much anxiety about in his critique of *Citizens United*.[46]

Oddly enough other liberal egalitarians appeared sensitive to these kinds of problems in a way that Dworkin wasn't. For instance, echoing our distinction between power and influence, Lani Guinier drew on decades of research on racial inequity to argue for major democratic reforms in the interest of procedural fairness. Rather than have a system where disparities in power led to wildly unequal opportunities to determine political outcomes, Guinier held that "a system is procedurally fair to the extent that it gives each participant an equal opportunity to influence [democratic] outcomes."[47] But the mature Rawls, deeply inspired by "radical democrats and socialists (and..Marx)[48]" was perhaps the most important to reach this conclusion. In *Justice as Fairness: A Restatement* he came to reject the idea that even robust welfarism was compatible

---

[44] See Brennan, Jason. *Against Democracy*. (Princeton, NJ: Princeton University Press, 2016).

[45] See Michel Foucault. The Archaeology of Knowledge, trans. A.M Sheridan Smith (London and New York, NY: Routledge, 2007).

[46] There is some overlap between this and Habermasian discourse ethics. See Jurgen Habermas. The Theory of Communicative Action Volume Two: Lifeworld and System-A Critique of Functionalist Reason, trans. Thomas McCarthy. (Boston, MA: Beacon Press, 1985).

[47] See Lani Guinier. *The Tyranny of the Majority: Fundamental Freedoms in Representative Democracy*. (New York, NY: The Free Press, 1995) at pg 156.

[48] See John Rawls. Justice as Fairness: A Restatement. (Cambridge, MA. The Belknap Press of Harvard University Press, 2001) at pg 148.

with the liberal principles of justice as fairness. This was because, among other things, disparities in economic wealth invariably led to inequalities in political power. This was true even where a state guaranteed formally equal political liberties. Beyond just entrenching equal rights to political liberties in the law, a just liberal state needed to ensure citizens got fair value from those political liberties. This would entail vast efforts to equalize disparities in political power arising from economic (and racial, gendered, and sexual[49]) subordination. As Rawls put it "given the lack of background justice and inequalities in income and wealth, there may develop a discouraged and depressed underclass many of whose members are chronically dependent on welfare. This underclass feels left out and does not participate in public political culture. …institutions must, from the outset, put in the hands of citizens generally, and not only of a few, sufficient productive means for them to be fully cooperating members of society on a footing of equality."[50]

For a Dworkinean partnership democracy to genuinely show equal respect to its members, it would need to take seriously this Guinier-Rawlsian argument for the importance of fair and equal value arising from political liberties. How to establish such conditions is beyond the scope of this book. However it is worth noting Rawls' pessimism that even a robust welfare state on the Scandinavian model would be insufficient. Given how far the United States and many countries are from even this minimally just society in 2023, there is a huge amount to be done.

Securing a Partnership Democracy Part III: Against *Rucho v Common Cause*

The urgency of making efforts to secure jurisprudential support for partnership democracy is highlighted by Supreme Court's ongoing willingness to attack the ideal of democratic equality. Nowhere was this better demonstrated than in the recent decision *Rucho v Common Cause*. Handed down in 2019, Dworkin was not alive to produce what would have surely been a scathing critique of the decision. However, it is not hard to guess what Dworkin would have had to say,.

---

[49] Unfortunately, until recently, many liberal egalitarians failed to take these forms of subordination sufficiently seriously.

[50] See John Rawls. *Justice as Fairness: A Restatement.* (Cambridge, MA. The Belknap Press of Harvard University Press, 2001) at pg 140.

The *Rucho* decision concerned whether the SCOTUS could review allegations of partisan gerrymandering and rectify them if discovered. In the cases at hand, such gerrymandering was taking place on a truly grotesque scale. In Maryland, the Democratic incumbents had redrawn districts so that—even though never winning more than 65 percent of the popular vote—they never the less regularly won 7 of 8 congressional districts. The Republicans in North Carolina were even more ambitious. Representative David Lewis, apparently deciding that such things are better left to him than voters, declared "I think electing Republicans is better than electing Democrats. So I drew this map to help foster what I think is better for the country." Despite only winning between 50–53 percent of the popular vote, the district redrawing resulted in the GOP winning 9–10 of 12–13 seats. Not content with this, Lewis lamented that he was forced to draw "the maps to give a partisan advantage to 10 Republicans and 3 Democrats because [I] d[o] not believe it['s] possible to draw a map with 11 Republicans and 2 Democrats."[51]

In *Rucho* the conservative Justices didn't even bother trying to deny that partisan gerrymandering was taking place, or that it had the effect of diluting the voting strength of supporters of the weakened party. They did insist that it "hardly follows from the principle that each person must have an equal say in the election of representatives that a person is entitled to have his political party achieve representation in some way commensurate to its share of statewide support."[52] The conservative Judges in fact insisted that the Framers understood that a degree of political involvement in districting was inevitable and that the question was only the ambiguous one of beyond what threshold did it become pernicious. But the more important objection was the Justices' insistence that they felt it was beyond the scope of the Court's expertise and right to determine how to resolve partisan gerrymandering, especially in the absence of any "neutral" criteria for what would be a fairer system. The majority highlighted how any criteria put forward would inherently be condemned by one party or another as unfair, and that it was unclear how much political motivation in drawing district lines is too much:

---

[51] *Rucho v. Common Cause*, No. 18–422, 588 U.S. (2019) at pg 4.
[52] *Rucho v. Common Cause*, No. 18–422, 588 U.S. (2019) at pg 20.

As an initial matter, it does not make sense to use criteria that will vary from State to State and year to year as the baseline for determining whether a gerrymander violates the Federal Constitution. The degree of partisan advantage that the Constitution tolerates should not turn on criteria offered by the gerrymanderers themselves. It is easy to imagine how different criteria could move the median map toward different partisan distributions. As a result, the same map could be constitutional or not depending solely on what the mapmakers said they set out to do. That possibility illustrates that the dissent's proposed constitutional test is indeterminate and arbitrary. Even if we were to accept the dissent's proposed baseline, it would return us to "the original unanswerable question (How much political motivation and effect is too much?)." Vieth, 541 U. S., at 296–297 (plurality opinion). Would twenty percent away from the median map be okay? Forty percent? Sixty percent? Why or why not? (We appreciate that the dissent finds all the unanswerable questions annoying, see post, at 22, but it seems a useful way to make the point.) The dissent's answer says it all: "This much is too much." Post, at 25–26. That is not even trying to articulate a standard or rule.[53]

In many respects, as Kagan's dissent points out, the epistemic ambiguity exploited in the majority decision seems disingenuous. Not least because both lower courts had been converging on clear criteria for adjudicating the fairness of districting, and because the different states had "(non-partisan) districting criteria as the baseline from which to measure partisan gerrymandering."[54] With due respect to Justice Kagan, this pays the conservative justices too much credit with regard to the integrity of their questioning. It is highly doubtful that a series of Ivy League educated Judges—some showered with all the relaxing luxuries Harlan Crow can provide—were not in a position to evaluate the relative neutrality of districting proposals which second-year political science undergraduates typically assess with acumen. Instead, the mode of questioning deployed by the majority reflects what Hirschman characterized as

[53] *Rucho v. Common Cause*, No. 18–422, <u>588 U.S.</u> (2019) at pgs 27–28.
[54] *Rucho v. Common Cause*, No. 18–422, <u>588 U.S.</u> (2019) at pg 25.

a rhetoric of "futility"[55] typically deployed by reactionaries.[56] The effect of presenting a line of seemingly unanswerable questions and surrounding them with pseudo-worldly lamentations that partisan politicking will always be with us, is to induce a sense of powerlessness in the face of entrenched social inequalities. By coupling this with its own mournful insistence that it personally disagrees with partisan gerrymandering but is not sure what the answer is, the majority effectively neuters aspirations for social change while insulating itself from the accurate charge of being the simps of power.

Dworkin's response to the *Rucho* decision would undoubtedly have been to applaud Kagan and the dissenting Justice's fortitude in not being badgered into submitting. He'd have replied that the best most principled interpretation of the First and Fourteenth Amendments naturally cannot support a political context where partisan redistricting produces such procedurally unfair results. The more basic issue isn't whether a citizen "is entitled to have his political party achieve representation in some way commensurate to its share of statewide support"—though that is important as a matter of representational fairness. The issue is if, by diluting their ability to influence electoral outcomes through packing and cracking, the law treats citizens as equal partners in a collective political project. And the answer is clearly no. Indeed, to hear Representative Lewis put it, the intention behind redistricting is to have the opposite effect: to privilege the electoral outcomes preferred by himself and his associates through diluting other's citizens' capacity to have an equal say and ensuring Republican victories. As Justice Kagan put it sharply one "might think that judgment best left to the American people."[57] But apparently, citizen's views are not what matters when it comes to the laws and policies which govern them and to which they are expected to submit to.

The *Rucho* case was an ideal circumstance where the SCOTUS could play a role in protecting the integrity of electoral laws through

---

[55] The futility rhetoric is typically the most effective in inducing a sense of progressive paralysis because, as Corey Robin stresses, it has a surface affinity for forms of structural critique common in left-circles.

[56] See Albert.O. Hirschman The Rhetoric of Reaction: Perversity, Futility, Jeopardy. (Cambridge, MA: The Belknap Pres of Harvard University Press, 1991).

[57] *Rucho v. Common Cause*, No. 18–422, <u>588</u> U.S. (2019) at pg 4.

constraining anti-democratic efforts, and consequently justifying its institutional existence by showing equal concern to citizens whose electoral voices are in effect being zoned out by procedural unfairness. Instead the conservative majority concluded that given its powerlessness and ignorance in the face of partisan gerrymandering, the solution to the noble crusade for democratic fairness has to be found at the state level. Which of course is tantamount to saying that partisan gerrymanderers should be responsible for eliminating the partisan gerrymandering which has benefited them thus far. Good luck.

What is all the more extraordinary is how strikingly the rhetoric of powerlessness in *Rucho* contrasts with the muscular confidence of *Citizens United*. In *Citizens United* the majority felt very confident in wildly speculating about the nirvana of free speech which would be created by licensing legal fiction to spend money and how this would be entirely free from political corruption. Yet when faced when transparent political corruption in a far more straightforward case with a long history of legal precedents behind it, the conservative majority was simply not sure what to do and retreated in the samsara of endless vacillation. It is a testament to how far the SCOTUS has gone in ceding the ideal of partnership democracy to plutocracy.

CONCLUSION

Dworkin's partnership view of democracy, consisting of citizens accorded equal respect and concern by law as they engage in a collective political enterprise, is a deeply inspiring one. From an American standpoint the tools it offers to advance a more egalitarian approach to law, and justice are extraordinary, as demonstrated in Dworkin's sharp critique of the most anti-democratic decision by the Supreme Court in recent memory. However, Dworkin's own understanding of partnership democracy is insufficiently egalitarian and democratic and requires greater attentiveness to disparities in economic power if it is to be fully convincing. It also requires extension to domains, like the workplace, that have historically been sidelined by liberal theorists. Fortunately, many of the tools to adequately rectify Dworkin's partnership view of democracy exist within the liberal egalitarian tradition, supplemented where necessary by insights from radical democrats and socialists.

Of course, disparities in economic power are not the only ones liberals must be deeply attentive to-especially in a country with as dark a history of racism as the United States. It's to these issues that we now turn.

CHAPTER 4

Racial Integration and Affirmative Action

Abstract This chapter dives into the thorny issues of race and racial equality in post-*Brown* America and beyond. We analyze Dworkin's complex thoughts on how to integrate a country long defined by white supremacism and segregation. The chapter then continues our application of Dworkinean jurisprudence through an analysis of the recent Supreme Court decisions on affirmative action.

Keyword Brown v Board of Topeka · White Supremacy · Racial Integration · Affirmative Action

The Legacy of *Brown v Board of Education*

The legacy of racism and racial discrimination remains among the most contentious and persistent issues dividing American society. The engagement of the courts, and especially the US Supreme Court, with this legacy is a familiar one. Often, the beginning of the liberal tradition in American law and the courts is traced to the case of *Brown v Board of Education of Topeka* in 1954.[1] In a unanimous decision, the Supreme

---

[1] *Brown v. Board of Education of Topeka*, 347 U.S. 483 (1954).

L. A. Jacobs and M. McManus, *Against Post-Liberal Courts and Justice*, Palgrave Studies in Classical Liberalism, https://doi.org/10.1007/978-3-031-45347-2_4

Court ruled that US state laws establishing racial segregation in public schools are unconstitutional and inherently unequal, reversing the "separate and equal" doctrine the court had embraced in 1896. Chief Justice Earl Warren noted in the Brown case that in the opinion of the entire court, "Today, education is perhaps the most important function of our local and state governments" (493). The effects in 1954 of racial segregation in public schools were, for Chief Justice Warren, immense. Warren famously wrote, "To separate [black children] from others of similar age and qualifications solely because of their race generates a feeling of inferiority as to their status in the community that may affect their hearts and minds in a way unlikely to ever be undone" (494).

The Brown opinion in 1954 paved the way for a series of subsequent decisions over the next two decades that reflected a constitutional commitment to the liberal principle of racial integration in public life. The extent of this commitment was visible in consistent support for major initiatives by the civil rights movement, directly impacting the everyday lives of Americans. The Supreme Court struck down laws that, for example, prohibited inter-racial marriages and created systemic barriers for African Americans in the workplace. Meanwhile, the federal government enacted monumental new legislation, most notably the *Civil Rights Act* of 1964 and the *Voting Rights Act* of 1965, that reinforced the vision of racial integration and created a new legal toolkit to challenge racism and racial discrimination in American society. The Supreme Court readily upheld the constitutionality of this new toolkit for the civil rights movement.

At the core of the vision of the civil rights legislation is the idea that persons should be treated as equals without regard to their racial identity. Martin Luther King Junior, in his "I have a Dream" speech in 1963, provided the most famous expression of this vision:

> When the architects of our republic wrote the magnificent words of the Constitution and the Declaration of Independence, they were signing a promissory note to which every American was to fall heir. This note was a promise that all men—yes, Black men as well as white men—would be guaranteed the unalienable rights of life, liberty and the pursuit of happiness. It is obvious today that America has defaulted on this promissory note insofar as her citizens of color are concerned... I have a dream that one day this nation will rise up and live out the true meaning of its creed: We hold these truths to be self-evident, that all men are created equal...

I have a dream that my four little children will one day live in a nation where they will not be judged by the color of their skin but by the content of their character.[2]

A half century later, the meaning and application of the civil rights vision with regard to racial identity remains contested in the American courts. Nowhere is this contest more evident or pressing than in the arguments in the post-liberal US Supreme Court over the constitutionality of race-sensitive affirmative action in admissions decisions at elite universities and colleges. In essence, these challenges to affirmative action are questioning the importance of the liberal commitment to racial integration in American society. The US Supreme Court's 2023 decision in the cases of *Students for Fair Admissions Inc. v. President and Fellows of Harvard College* and *Students for Fair Admissions Inc. v. University of North Carolina* that after fifty years, race-sensitive affirmative action is suddenly unconstitutional is a clear signal of the dismal plight of racial integration in post-liberal institutions.

THE LIBERAL COMMITMENT TO RACIAL INTEGRATION

The liberal legacy of the *Brown* decision and arguably civil rights legislation is an expanding circle of integration for targeted historically marginalized communities in educational institutions, beginning with racial minorities but quickly extending to other equity seeking groups including women, persons with disabilities, the gay and lesbian communities, indigenous populations, and more recently other sexual identities such as Trans individuals.[3] This legacy spilled over into other major public institutions including especially the racial integration of the American military.

In practice, however, racial integration did not just happen seamlessly and without incident in the 1960s once the civil rights movement had some successes and overt barriers of racism were removed. President Lyndon Johnson insightfully observed in 1965 the limitations of being insensitive to racial differences when embracing fair equality of opportunity,

---

[2] Martin Luther King Jr, "I have a Dream", March on Washington, August 28, 1963. https://www.npr.org/2010/01/18/122701268/i-have-a-dream-speech-in-its-entirety.

[3] Martha Minow. In *Browns Wake*, 1st edn. (Oxford University Press, 2010).

You do not take a person who, for years, has been hobbled by chains and liberate him, bring him up to the starting line of a race and then say, 'You are free to compete with all the others,' and still justly believe that you have been completely fair. Thus it is not enough just to open the gates of opportunity. All our citizens must have the ability to walk through these gates.[4]

President Johnson's central insight is that remedying for racial disadvantage and promoting fairer racial integration is a forward-looking challenge, which must be sensitive to race and racial differences.

One important public policy solution to meet this challenge has been the adoption of race-sensitive affirmative action. Affirmative action should be understood as a program, policy, or practice to advance racial integration in society that seeks to remedy significant disadvantage or underrepresentation of members of certain racial, ethnic, or other groups through measures that are not color-blind but rather take group membership or identity into account.[5] Although affirmative action has sometimes been implemented to address concerns about the underrepresentation of women or persons with disabilities, the highest profile use of affirmative action has been to remedy for the ongoing impacts of systemic racism, especially by colleges and universities, on achieving racial integration in the United States.

Wide-spread race-sensitive affirmative action in admissions decisions for colleges and universities first emerged in the 1970s. In essence, some colleges and universities began to consider the race of applicants when making decisions about who to admit into their freshman cohort, medical school, or faculty of law, for the purpose of achieving racial integration and diversity. Black and Hispanic applicants were intended to be the principal target for affirmative action by recruitment and admissions offices since those groups were typically underrepresented in colleges and universities. Not surprising, some applicants from other racial groups, especially those who identity as white, feel that race-sensitive affirmative action treats them unfairly.

[4] Lyndon Johnson, "To Fulfill these Rights", Howard University Commencement Address, June 4, 1965. https://www.presidency.ucsb.edu/documents/commencement-address-howard-university-fulfill-these-rights.

[5] Lesley Jacobs, *Pursuing Equal Opportunities* (New York, NY: Cambridge University Press, 2004), p. 116.

The most powerful objection to affirmative action is that it is unfair because it takes the race or ethnicity of individuals into account, and for some individuals, most notably those in the "white majority," their racial identity counts as a negative factor in admission decisions. Affirmative action is said to violate the civil rights of those individuals because they are in effect being discriminated against based on their race or ethnicity— contrary to Martin Luther King Jr's civil rights movement-inspired dream. In effect, rather than advance fair racial integration, affirmative action hinders it.

In a series of cases beginning almost twenty-five years after the *Brown* decision, the US Supreme Court has consistently, albeit narrowly, upheld the constitutionality of a certain type of race-sensitive affirmative action program in college and university admission decisions.[6] In competitions for scarce good such as university places, affirmative action programs are fair when they allow the race or ethnicity of certain targeted groups to count as a *plus factor* for individual applicants in the allocation of those goods. This use of race as a plus factor should be carefully differentiated from a *quota* program where a certain proportion or share of university places are set aside for racial minorities. For the past fifty years, it has been settled law for the Supreme Court that plus factor race-based affirmative action programs are constitutional.

In November 2022, the Supreme Court heard oral arguments in a pair of cases brought against Harvard University and the University of South Carolina alleging that race-sensitive affirmative action in admissions decisions are unconstitutional because they unfairly discriminate against White and Asian applicants. Many of the objections to affirmative action raised in these cases, *Students for Fair Admissions Inc. v. President and Fellows of Harvard College* and *Students for Fair Admissions Inc. v. University of North Carolina,* are similar to ones heard in the previous cases. But this time the Supreme Court hearing these cases is decidedly post-liberal.

---

[6] *Regents of the University of California v. Bakke,* 438 U.S. 265 (1978); *Grutter v. Bollinger,* 539 U.S. 306 (2003).
  Fisher v. University of Texas, 579 U.S. 365 (2016).

THE CASE AGAINST RACE-SENSITIVE AFFIRMATIVE ACTION

What is the 2023 case against race-sensitive affirmative action brought by the plaintiff in *Students for Fair Admissions Inc. v. President and Fellows of Harvard College* and *Students for Fair Admissions Inc. v. University of North Carolina?* Their argument begins with an appealing, albeit contested, interpretation of the Brown decision by the Supreme Court, which is described as "the single most important and greatest decision in this Court's history."[7] The Supreme Court held in Brown, according to the plaintiffs, that the Constitution denies "any authority ... to use race as a factor in affording educational opportunities."[8] The principal problem with racial segregation in public schools in the 1950s was that it used race to limit educational opportunities for African American children, where education was recognized to be the pathway for upward social mobility and greater racial integration. The Supreme Court in 1954 unanimously determined that this use of race is unconstitutional. For the plaintiff in 2023, the important legacy of the Brown decision is the embrace of a "color-blind constitution" by the Supreme Court since 1954, one that does not allow for race-sensitive policies and practices to be a fair way to advance racial integration in our institutions of education.[9] In effect, race-sensitive policies and practices are allegedly contrary to the bedrock constitutional principle of equal protection for all under law.

This interpretation of Brown has significant implications for race-sensitive affirmative action. When race-sensitive affirmative action is used in admissions decisions by universities like Harvard or University of North Carolina, the plaintiff reasons that fundamentally this is similar to racial segregation in public schools in the sense that race is a factor that impacts the educational opportunities of applicants to those universities. In fact, these universities readily acknowledge that in their affirmative action programs race is a "plus factor" in admission decisions. But logically, given the holding of Brown, any such use of race as a factor in affording

---

[7] Students for Fair Admissions Brief, 20–1199 21–707 SFFA (May 22, 2022), Supreme Court Docket, p. 47. https://www.supremecourt.gov/DocketPDF/20/20-1199/222 325/20220502145522418_20-1199%2021-707%20SFFA%20Brief%20to%20file%20final. pdf.

[8] Students for Fair Admissions Brief, 20–1199 21–707 SFFA (May 22, 2022), p. 47.

[9] Students for Fair Admissions Brief, 20–1199 21–707 SFFA (May 22, 2022), p. 5.

educational opportunities is unconstitutional, including race-sensitive admissions decisions at Harvard and North Carolina.

There is another important dimension to the case against race-sensitive affirmative action by the plaintiff in *Students for Fair Admissions Inc. v. President and Fellows of Harvard College* and *Students for Fair Admissions Inc. v. University of North Carolina* that also draws on Brown. At the outset of the chapter, we noted that for the Supreme Court in 1954 it was significant that racial segregation in public schools caused serious and long-lasting harm for African American children. Similarly, it is argued that race-sensitive affirmative action by universities harms racialized students, especially Asian American students. The harms include: "anti-Asian stereotyping, race-obsessed campuses, declines in ideological diversity, and more."[10] Like in Brown, these tangible harms are alleged to be the basis for urgency on the part of the Supreme Court to end race-sensitive affirmative action by universities across the country.

Dworkin's Defense of Race-Sensitive Affirmative Action

Among constitutional law experts in the United States, Ronald Dworkin was one of the most consistent and vocal defenders of the use of race-sensitive affirmative action measures by American colleges and universities for more than fifty years. For Dworkin, it was fundamental to recognize that affirmative action is not being undertaken to remedy for past racial injustices—it is not in this sense backward looking—but rather to advance racial integration and equal opportunity in the future—in this sense it is forward looking. In effect, he echoed President Johnson's insight about systemic racism and the barriers it creates to furthering racial integration.

For Dworkin, the record is clear that affirmative action works to strengthen racial integration and equality of opportunity for all.[11] Black undergraduate students who enrolled in a university or college with race-sensitive affirmative action made more money after they graduated than if they had gone to school somewhere else. They also report higher satisfaction with their university experience and subsequent career choices. These

---

[10] Students for Fair Admissions Brief, 20–1199 21–707 SFFA (May 22, 2022), p. 48.

[11] Ronald Dworkin, *Sovereign Virtue* (Cambridge, MA: Harvard University Press, 2000), pp. 386–407. See also Jacobs, *Pursuing Equal Opportunities*, Chapter Five.

individuals are also more likely to take on leadership roles in the communities where they live. At the community level, race-sensitive affirmative action has had the effect of producing more Black physicians, lawyers, professors, and business executives. At the same time, white and Asian Americans who attended universities and colleges with race-sensitive affirmative action are more inclusive of racial diversity in their daily lives. And a large number—two-thirds—identify their student experiences as playing an important role.

The core legal argument of the plaintiff in *Students for Fair Admissions Inc. v. President and Fellows of Harvard College* and *Students for Fair Admissions Inc. v. University of North Carolina* is that race-sensitive affirmative action denies equal protection for all and harms white and Asian applicants who seek to enroll in undergraduate programs at Harvard or University of North Carolina. How would Dworkin respond?

For Ronald Dworkin, it is fundamental to recognize the limited reach of the constitutional principle of equal protection:

> The equal protection clause is violated, not whenever some group has lost an important decision..., but when its loss results from a special vulnerability to prejudice or hostility or stereotype and its consequent diminished standing–its second-class citizenship—in the political community. The clause does not guarantee each citizen that [they] will benefit equally from every...decision.[12]

In the *Brown* decision, the Supreme Court found that the decision to implement racial segregation in public schools violated the equal protection clause because it treated Black students as second-class citizens, stemming from hostility and prejudice.

The broader point is that for Dworkin the constitutional principle of equal protection does not rule out or prohibit all race-sensitive decision making, but rather only race-sensitive decision making that stems from prejudice, vulnerability, hostility, or stereotype. Some race-sensitive decision making can have more positive aspirations, as the Supreme Court has consistently recognized in upholding certain provisions of the 1965 *Voting Rights Act*. The problem with the idea of a "color-blind constitution" is that it is too overly simplistic with a proposed blanket prohibition of any race-sensitivity. This prohibition fails to recognize that,

---

[12] Dworkin, *Sovereign Virtue*, p. 411.

for example, for many African Americans race is an integral positive part of their personal self-identification and their everyday lived reality. It can be tied to cultural pride and a remarkable history of overcoming adversity and resilience. To embrace color-blindness amounts to not only curtailing prejudice and discrimination, but also white-washing the saliency of race in the unique lived reality of African Americans. If you think about the broader context of King's I have a dream speech in 1963, it envisioned a constitution that not just sought the elimination of prejudice and racial discrimination but also recognition of the distinct positive contributions of African Americans as a people to the United States.[13] That speech is tantamount to a rejection—not an embrace—of a color-blind constitution.

It may well be the case that without race-sensitive affirmative action, more white or Asian American applicants would be admitted to Harvard and the University of North Carolina. This may be a genuine loss for some of those prospective applicants. But that loss is a violation of the constitutional principle of equal protection only when it stems from hostility or vulnerability or amounts to treatment as a second-class citizen. Does affirmative action at these two universities reflect hostility or prejudice toward white or Asian American students?

There are other ways in which applicants to universities like Harvard or University of North Carolina lose out. For example, both universities provide preferential treatment for elite student athletes. Many prospective white or Asian American applicants lose out because they are not elite athletes. Is the preferential treatment of elite athletes a violation of the equal protection principle? Harvard, like many other private universities, also has preferential treatment for children of alumnae. Could this preferential treatment be construed as hostility or prejudice toward some prospective applicants simply because there is a loss for them? The answer is of course no, even though this further enables the extraordinary concentration of access to elite schools in the hands of the already staggeringly wealthy. The same reasoning applies to race-sensitive affirmative action. The fact that there may be a loss for some white or Asian American applicants is not sufficient on its own to conclude that there is hostility, vulnerability, or stereotyping.

---

[13] Jacobs, *Pursuing Equal Opportunities*, Ch. 6.

The onus is on the plaintiff in the plaintiff in *Students for Fair Admissions Inc. v. President and Fellows of Harvard College* and *Students for Fair Admissions Inc. v. University of North Carolina* to demonstrate hostility, vulnerability, or stereotyping toward white and Asian American students. In the 1954 Brown case, the Supreme Court was persuaded that racial segregation of schools resulted in a very substantial loss for Black children and that the policy did stem from prejudice. There is scant evidence of something similar in the case of race-sensitive affirmative action in decision making in colleges and universities.

The US Supreme Court's Decision in 2023

In June 2023, the Supreme Court decided in a 6–3 opinion that race-sensitive affirmative action is a violation of the fourteenth amendment, overturning in practice a series of decisions over the previous fifty years where it upheld the constitutionality of the practice in admissions decisions by colleges and universities. Like with *Roe v. Wade*, this reversal by the Supreme Court reflects a major departure from what a liberal court had done.

Chief Justice John Roberts, writing for the majority of justice on the Supreme Court in *Students for Fair Admissions Inc. v. President and Fellows of Harvard College* and *Students for Fair Admissions Inc. v. University of North Carolina*, noted that since the Brown decision in 1954:

> this Court continued to vindicate the Constitution's pledge of racial equality...Our cases had thus "consistently denied the constitutionality of measures which restrict the rights of citizens on account of race."...These decisions reflect the "core purpose" of the Equal Protection Clause: "do[ing] away with all governmentally imposed discrimination based on race." ...We have recognized that repeatedly. "The clear and central purpose of the Fourteenth Amendment was to eliminate all official state sources of invidious racial discrimination in the States."[14]

---

[14] 600 U. S. ____ (2023), 13–14.

And then Chief Justice Roberts asserts, "Eliminating racial discrimination means eliminating all of it."[15] In his assessment, race-sensitive affirmative action for Black, Hispanic, and indigenous students amounts to racial discrimination against Asian American and white students, and should therefore be eliminated.

Chief Justice Roberts expresses the belief that previous decisions by the Court permitted race-sensitive college admissions decisions only when they serve a valid purpose, do not use race as a stereotype or negative, and are not a permanent part of the admissions process.[16] In his view, race-sensitive admissions at both Harvard and the University of North Carolina fail to meet any of these conditions.

Surprisingly, the majority opinion systematically challenges what had been well-established legal justification for race-sensitive college admissions for two generations, in effect, the educational benefits of diversity in the university undergraduate body, finding that there is nothing here that is "measurable and concrete enough to permit judicial review."[17]

Chief Justice Roberts explains,

> the interests [the universities] view as compelling cannot be subjected to meaningful judicial review. Harvard identifies the following educational benefits that it is pursuing: (1) "train- ing future leaders in the public and private sectors"; (2) pre- paring graduates to "adapt to an increasingly pluralistic so- ciety"; (3) "better educating its students through diversity"; and (4) "producing new knowledge stemming from diverse outlooks."... the question in this context is not one of no diversity or of some: it is a question of degree. How many fewer leaders Harvard would create without racial preferences, or how much poorer the education at Harvard would be, are inquiries no court could resolve.[18]

In effect, the current majority of Justices on the Supreme Court are challenging the very familiar business case for diversity that has been a long

[15] 600 U. S. ____ (2023), 15.
[16] 22.
[17] 7.
[18] 600 U. S. ____ (2023), 23.

researched and measured by many economists and other social scientists—findings that are widely accepted in America's business community.[19]

As we noted above, Dworkin engaged this extensive research, finding in it precisely answers to the kinds of questions that the Court appears to believe are unanswerable. Dworkin found in the empirical research that Black individuals are also more likely to take on leadership roles in the communities where they live. At the community level, race-sensitive affirmative action has had the effect of producing more Black leaders from physicians, lawyers, and professors to business executives and politicians. At the same time, white and Asian Americans who attended universities and colleges with race-sensitive affirmative action are more inclusive of racial diversity and supportive of minority leaders in their daily lives. Like with so much of Dworkin's work, it appears like he very much anticipated and dismantled the line of reasoning that the post-liberal Supreme Court is pursuing.

Undeniably, the sorts of questions Chief Justice Roberts identifies require sophisticated research methods to answer, including randomized control trials, interventions, and advanced statistics. But these methods have been readily utilized in the scholarly affirmative action research, and indeed recognized as having validity in earlier decisions by the Supreme Court on race-based affirmative action.[20] And in other types of legal cases involving race, especially voting rights cases stemming from the 1965 *Voting Rights Act*, the Supreme Court has been a pioneer in utilizing these sorts of methodologies in their judicial review.

There is something similarly puzzling in Chief Justice Robert's claim that admissions decisions that give positive weight to some applicants for their racial identity are inherently creating a negative factor for the racial identity of other applicants. He stresses under the Equal Protection Clause, race can never be used as a "negative" and more specifically "an individual's race may never be used against him in the admissions process."[21] It is readily acknowledged that universities and colleges allege that they are not using the race of White or Asian applicants against them

---

[19] See for example, Harvard Business Review, *On Diversity: HBR's 10 Must-Read on Diversity* (Cambridge,MA: Harvard Business School, 2019).

[20] The seminal study is William Bowen & Derek Bok, *The Shape of the River: Long-Term Consequences of Considering Race in College and University Admissions, Twentieth Anniversary Edition* (Princeton, NJ: Princeton University Press, 2018).

[21] 27.

in the admissions. But Chief Justice Roberts finds that this simply is not the case, noting "College admissions are zero-sum. A benefit provided to some applicants but not to others necessarily advantages the former group at the expense of the latter."[22] The logic by the Chief Justice here is clearly circular in the sense that he insists that the Equal Protections Clause always prohibits race being utilized as a negative factor in admissions decisions, so when he asks whether the Equal Protections Clause allows for race as a plus factor, while starting from the assumption that if race is a plus factor for some applicants, it is also by necessity a negative factor for other applicants. Given his initial assumption, it is always going to be case that the conclusion is that race as a plus factor is not allowed by the Equal Protections Clause.

Dworkin again provides important insights on this issue. For Dworkin, what the Equal Protections Clause prohibits is race as a negative factor only when it stems from hostility or vulnerability or amounts to treatment as a second-class citizen. In *Brown*, the problem with the segregated public schools was that they treated black students as second-class citizens, as did so many other racially segregated public facilities. The real test that Chief Justice Roberts should have applied in the *Students for Fair Admissions Inc. v. President and Fellows of Harvard College* and *Students for Fair Admissions Inc. v. University of North Carolina* was whether or not White or Asian applicants were being treated as second-class citizens. There is room here for serious debate and differences of opinion—maybe these two universities genuinely do marginalize Asian students. There is an opportunity to have a robust discussion about the complex and evolving nature of systemic racism in America, including listening to the important voices from Critical Race Theory. But alas this is not the test that Chief Justice Roberts applied nor is it the discussion he engaged in. Instead, through his circular logic he arrived at the conclusion that race as plus factor must be a negative factor for White and Asian applicants without ever engaging in a serious conversation about racism, in much the same way that he does not acknowledge all of the well-established research on the value of diversity and how to measure its impact on American society.

[22] 27.

CONCLUSION

As we noted at the outset of this chapter, the unanimous decision in *Brown v Board of Education* by the US Supreme Court in 1954 is often identified as the clear emergence of the liberal ascendence in the federal courts. The 2023 decision by the Supreme Court to strike down the practice of race-sensitive admissions decisions in the twin cases of *Students for Fair Admissions Inc. v. President and Fellows of Harvard College* and *Students for Fair Admissions Inc. v. University of North Carolina* is arguably the bookend to end this era. At its core, the Brown decision was a reflection of a national commitment to improving racial integration. And the 2023 decision is a reflection of a Supreme Court that no longer shares the commitment to improving racial integration and creating a more egalitarian society.

The aftermath of the court's race-based affirmative decision has had consequences that were likely not anticipated by those who advocate for a post-liberal court and justice. In the same way that the aftermath of *Dobbs v. Jackson Women's Health Organization* has been a political backlash against conservative politicians, there has been increased scrutiny of legacy preferential treatment in admissions for alumnae—so-called legacy admissions—in private colleges and universities. Legacy admissions have long been recognized as contributors to significant socio-economic inequality in the United States. As the American Civil Liberties Union recently explained, "Many of these students compete for limited spots at universities that use "legacy status" as a factor when weighing admissions—a practice that disproportionately gives preference to white and wealthy student applicants whose family member is an alumni of the college or university they're applying to. Ending these legacy admissions practices is a critical step that can help address long-standing disparities and inequality in higher education while increasing access for underrepresented students who have been historically shut out."[23] Likely, over the next couple of years, more and more universities and college will end legacy admissions as a result of the Supreme Court's decision in *Students for Fair Admissions Inc. v. President and Fellows of Harvard College* and *Students for*

---

[23] https://www.aclu.org/news/racial-justice/how-ending-legacy-admissions-can-help-achieve-greater-education-equity#:~:text=Legacy%20preferences%20reinforce%20long%20standing,to%20resources%20and%20institutional%20connections.

Fair Admissions Inc. v. University of North Carolina—an outcome that will likely improve equal opportunities for all.

CHAPTER 5

Pregnancy, Life, and the *Dobbs* Decision

Abstract This chapter looks at Dworkin's deep ruminations on the question of life's value and dignity in the context of debates around abortion and euthanasia. This demonstrates the expanse and frequent profundity of Dworkinean liberalism, belying the post-liberal critique of the liberal tradition as incapable of offering guidance on the most painful existential questions. The chapter concludes with an extensive and critical analysis of the *Dobbs* decision, which has historically rolled back abortion rights in the United States.

A Life Worth Living

The life of a single human organism commands respect and protection, then, no matter in what form or shape, because of the complex creative investment it represents and because of our wonder at the divine or evolutionary processes that produce new lives from old ones, at the processes of nation and community and language through which a human being will come to absorb and continue hundreds of generations of cultures and forms of life and value, and finally when mental life has begin and flourishes, at the process of internal personal creation and judgement by which a person will make a remake himself, a mysterious, inescapable process in which we each participate, and which is therefore the most powerful and inevitably source of empathy and communion we have with every other

L. A. Jacobs and M. McManus, *Against Post-Liberal Courts and Justice*, Palgrave Studies in Classical Liberalism, https://doi.org/10.1007/978-3-031-45347-2_5

creature who faces the same frightening challenge. The horror we feel in the willful destruction of a human life reflects our shared inarticulate sense of the intrinsic importance of each of these dimensions of investment.

Ronald Dworkin, *Life's Dominion*

Life is something most of us consider rather important. This makes it both shocking and unsurprising that matters of life and death have become so central to both American politics and the courts. Shocking because the argument that life has value if anything does could only be contended by the most marginal nihilists. Unsurprising because, even though everyone would agree that life has value (or, if you're Steve Bannon, the life with the right skin color) there is very little agreement on the source of this value. Nor is there any agreement on what modes of existence best reflect the conviction that life has value. For many religious citizens, life has value through its alignment with a higher transcendent order—whether that be narrativized through by conceiving humanity as the children of God, or participants in the cycle of samsara, or even regarding God himself as becoming human out of love for his creation. So deep does this conviction run that, for many religious citizens, it becomes impossible and even threatening to conceive life as gaining its value from any other source. This religious view is obviously disputed by those who've embraced more materialist ontologies, and regard any notion of a transcendent religious realm with skepticism and even incredulity. Yet they too will insist that life is sacred; indeed, for socialist atheists like Martin Hagglund, it is only through being finite and material that life's transience becomes precious and distinctive. Like a magnificent performance of Beethoven's 9th or Kendrick Lamar's "Duckworth" that fades with the last note, life is made worthwhile through being only for a while.[1]

Much of Dworkin's work is taken up with these profound questions, whether in the form of life's worth or the even broader questions of human dignity and the "unity of value."[2] While, as we've seen, Dworkin

---

[1] See Martin Hagglund. *This Life: Secular Faith and Spiritual Freedom.* (London, UK: Penguin Pantheon Books, 2019).

[2] See Salman Khurshid, Lokendra Malik and Veronica Rodriguez-Blanco. *Dignity in the Legal and Political Philosophy of Ronald Dworkin.* (Oxford, UK: Oxford University Press, 2018).

was very capable of deliberating on these topics from an abstract "outside in" perspective his most affecting ruminations on life and its value no doubt came when he was proceeding from the "inside out."[3] This included his extensive treatments of abortion, euthanasia, and other painful topics which have continued to dominate headlines and politics in the United States in the years since Dworkin's passing.

In this chapter we make the case that Dworkin offers very useful guides for how to organize progressive arguments for rights to abortion and to doctor assisted suicide. Most importantly, Dworkin's rare-among-liberals moral seriousness is able to convey the gravity of the issues at play in a manner which makes them very appealing in responding to the pathos of the post-liberal religious right. This is especially important in blunting the accusation that liberal arguments for abortion and doctor assisted suicide fail to respect the sanctity of life in their commitment to a doctrine of nihilistic permissiveness and hedonic gratification. Dworkin's ability to weave rights to abortion and euthanasia into a moral argument about individual freedom, dignity, and the good life make them invaluable in rebutting this bad faith charge.

ABORTION, OR, THE VALUE OF LIFE'S BEGINNING

Few arguments have galvanized American's political imagination more than abortion. Indeed, for many on the religious right abortion is treated as a matter of existential urgency as a moral wrong comparable to genocide. Indeed, such polemical and even apocalyptic language is hardly unseen even among contemporary post-liberal intellectuals. In his *Common Good Constitutionalism* Adrian Vermeule evokes a contest of competing theologies when he describes abortion as "one of the holiest sacraments"[4] of progressive human rights. In *Resurrecting the Idea of a Christian Society* R.R Reno describes abortion as flowing from the view that "morality, like sex, is socially constructed" which reaches the "point of denying reality."[5] This is despite the fact that, as theologian

---

[3] See Ronald Dworkin. *Life's Dominion: An Argument About Abortion, Euthanasia, and Individual Freedom.* (New York, NY: Vintage Books, 1994) at pg 29.

[4] See Adrian Vermeule. *Common Good Constitutionalism.* (Cambridge, UK: Polity Press, 2022) at pg 122.

[5] See R.R Reno. *Resurrecting the Idea of a Christian Society.* (New York, NY: Perseus Distribution, 2016) at pg 19.

Obery Hendricks observes, the Biblical and theological arguments for and against abortion are actually rather complex and by no means conform to the one-dimensional position staked out by American evangelicals.[6]

On the other front, for many feminist advocates abortion is about far more even than securing rights to reproductive freedom for women. It concerns the precarious treatment of women as equal citizens entitled to legal autonomy, with a plurality of justices in *Casey* famously linking abortion to an expressive individualist conception of human liberty. Stating that at "the heart of liberty is the right to define one's own concept of existence, of meaning, of the universe, and of the mystery of human life. Beliefs about these matters could not define the attributes of personhood were they formed under compulsion of the State."[7] This is to say nothing of the more radically feminist arguments, which stress that abortion needs to be situated in a patriarchal genealogy. For much of recorded history women's subordination was justified in no small part by the need to undervalue reproductive labor even while profiting from it.[8]

One of the difficulties in settling such a high octane debate is the way it links debates about the value of life to more descriptive metaphysical and meta-ethical questions about how the fetus can be adequately described. This is often misconstrued as a question about the "humanity" or "life" of the fetus, which in fact has never been at issue. No sophisticated defender of abortion has ever denied that a fetus is genetically "human" or that it is biologically alive.[9] Typically the higher order debates turn on whether a living human fetus is always already a moral "person" fully entitled to the normal rights to life guaranteed to all persons, a potential "person" with interests and rights to realize that potentiality,[10] or a collection of reproductive cells with no such rights until a certain threshold of development has passed. Some feminists, such as Judith Jarvis Thomson, would

---

[6] See Obery Hendricks. *Christians Against Christianity: How Right-Wing Evangelicals Are Destroying Our Nation and Our Faith.* (Boston, MA: Beacon Press, 2021) at pgs 106–114.

[7] *Planned Parenthood v. Casey*, 505 U.S. 833 (1992) at pg 851.

[8] See Catherine MacKinnon. *Towards a Feminist Theory of the State.* (Cambridge, MA: Harvard University Press, 1989).

[9] We can't think of any trenchant critic of abortion who wouldn't argue that a fetus was human or alive, so the inverse position seems less worthy of discussion.

[10] For a well known iteration of this argument see John Finnis. *Natural Law and Natural Rights: Second Edition.* (Oxford, UK: Oxford University Press, 2011).

argue that even if one could demonstrate that a fetus was a person entitled to normal rights to life that needn't outweigh the mother's equally compelling right to bodily autonomy. In her compelling thought experiment, Thomson asks us to imagine a violinist who is surgically attached without consent to another on whom he becomes dependent for life. Thomson points out that few would argue that the violinist has a right to remain surgically attached to another, even if that is necessary to conserve their life, since one's right to bodily autonomy trumps another's right to use our body to preserve themselves. Though even she admits that arguments for abortion become less appealing the closer a fetus comes to viability outside the mother.[11]

Dworkin's inspired move is to recognize both the irresolvable nature of these metaphysical and meta-ethical problems, and to acknowledge their central moral importance to disputants on all sides. For Dworkin, both critics and proponents of abortion miss the point when they deliberate on whether a fetus is a person and whether it is moral to terminate it. In his words, they adopt a "detached" view about the intrinsic sacredness of life rather than a "derivative" view that human life only becomes sacred because it is a condition for personhood. Dworkin claims "almost everyone shares, explicitly or intuitively, the idea that human life has objective, intrinsic value that is quite independent of its personal value for anyone, and disagreement about the right interpretation of that shared idea is the actual nerve of the great debate about abortion. For that reason, the debate is even more important to most people than an argument about whether a fetus is a person would be, for it goes deeper-into different conceptions of the value and point of human lie and the meaning and character of human death."[12] Dworkin insists that this can be seen in the more cool approaches to abortion witnesses in less heated moments, where very few anti-abortion activists would deny that abortion becomes more permissible in cases of incest, rape, or when birth would threaten the mother's health, and very few pro-abortion activists would in fact dismiss the choice to terminate a fetus as unimportant or even a matter for celebration. For Dworkin:

---

[11] See Judis Jarvis Thomson. "A Defense of Abortion." *Philosophy and Public Affairs,* Vol 1, No. 1.

[12] See Ronald Dworkin. *Life's Dominion: An Argument About Abortion, Euthanasia, and Individual Freedom.* (New York, NY: Vintage Books, 1994) at pg 67.

The life of a single human organism commands respect and protection then, no matter in what shape or form, because of the complex creative investment it represents and because of our wonder at the divine or evolutionary processes that produce new life from old ones. . - . The horror we feel in the willful destruction of a human life reflects our shared inarticulate sense of the intrinsic importance of each of these dimensions of investment.[13]

Dworkin then observes that precisely because disputes about the value of lie are of such central importance to the individuals impacted by them, they can be mobilized into a liberal argument that the state should refrain from imposing a uniform view on citizens. Precisely because decisions of the value of life are of intense religious/spiritual importance to individuals, it must be left to individuals to decide how to approach them.

Dworkin finds support for this view in his moral reading of the American constitution, which he holds denies a fetus constitutes a constitutional person with interests and rights which the law must protect. This reflects Dworkin's broader argument that the abortion issues truly turn on how to respect the sanctity of life rather than the personhood of the fetus. Dworkin then goes on to argue that since the American constitution does not acknowledge the constitutional personhood of a fetus; or as he puts it elsewhere "whether abortion is murder does not depend...on whether a fetus is a human being at some very early point after conception-of course it is-but on whether it has interests and so rights to protect those interests at that early stage."[14] Consequently the legal question then becomes what the most integral reading of the Constitution would be concerning whether the state should intervene on one side or another of debates about what constitutes the proper form of religious and spiritual respect for the sacredness of life? Here his answer is the American constitution clearly adopts the liberal view that equal citizens must have the liberty to reach such judgments for themselves. Indeed, he stressed that the "*Bill of Rights* places more emphasis on individual liberty, than does any other constitution." As if anticipating our post-*Dobbs* world, Dworkin argues it would be a "bleak day in American constitutional history" if *Roe vs Wade*

---

[13] See Ronald Dworkin. *Life's Dominion: An Argument About Abortion, Euthanasia, and Individual Freedom.* (New York, NY: Vintage Books, 1994) at pg 84.

[14] See Ronald Dworkin. *Is Democracy Possible Here?: Principles for a New Political Debate.* (Princeton, NJ: Princeton University Press, 2006) at pg 79.

was overturned for it "would mean that American citizens were no longer secure in their freedom to follow their own reflective convictions in the most person, conscience-driven, and religious decisions many of them will ever make."[15]

EUTHANASIA, OR, THE VALUE OF LIFE'S END

Camus once said that the only truly vexing philosophical problem is that of suicide. One could also reframe this as the question of Silenus: would we have been better off to have never been born, or at minimum to have the good fortune to die quickly? Most of us tend to ignore or reject such moribund questions when opiated by the glow of life's bloom. But they return with pointed vengeance when decay takes hold and we recognize, like Ivan Ilyich, that death—a necessary end—will come to us all. In these painful circumstances the question of how to live well becomes inextricably tied with how to die well; recognizing the death is not the ceasing but the conclusion of our lives.

These kinds of universally existential concerns pervade Dworkin's ruminations on euthanasia, many of which approximate a literary rather than an analytical tenor. This includes graphic tragedy of the sort one more associates with Foucault or Nietzsche than the genteel liberal jurist. Dworkin observes that every day, "rational people all over the world plead to be allowed to die. Sometimes they plead for others to kill them Some of them are drying already, many in great pain, like Lillian Boyes, a seventy-year old Englishwoman who was dying rom a terrible form of rheumatoid arthritis so painful that even the most powerful painkillers left her in agony, screaming when her son touched her hand with his finger."[16] Later he observes that "we live our whole lives in the shadow of death; it is also true that we die in the shadow of our whole lives. Death's central horror is oblivion-the terrifying, absolute dying of the light. But oblivion is not all there is to death; if it were, people would not worry so much about whether their technical, biological lives continue after they have become unconscious and the void has begun, after the light is already dead forever. Death has dominion because it is not only

---

[15] See Ronald Dworkin. *Life's Dominion: An Argument About Abortion, Euthanasia, and Individual Freedom.* (New York, NY: Vintage Books, 1994) at pg 172.

[16] See Ronald Dworkin. *Life's Dominion: An Argument About Abortion, Euthanasia, and Individual Freedom.* (New York, NY: Vintage Books, 1994) at pg 179.

the start of northing but the end of everything, and how we think and talk about dying-the emphasis we put on dying with 'dignity'-show how important it is that life ends appropriately, that death keeps faith with the way we want to have lived."[17]

This point is crucial in understanding Dworkin's support for the right to die. Where Dworkin expresses regret that abortion is a waste of life's beginning, he becomes appropriately existential when ruminating on the question of euthanasia. This is subtly different than the question of abortion, which entails precluding all possibilities for a fetus before it becomes autonomous. Death on the other hand, whether natural or chosen, is not just about the closing off of future possibilities—though it is that, which is why premature death is a great tragedy. Death is the final opportunity to affirm one's life in a dignified manner. In many respects the problem of death can be meaningfully compared to Dworkin's more strictly legal concern with the integrity of the law or a chain novel. The neverending story of law's empire is made richer through ensuring our most recent cases make the best of what comes before. By contrast, death is the last opportunity to say something about life, much as a "play's last scene or a poem's last stanza" bears on the entire work.[18] One may add that this may well be why tragedy so often resonates more than comedy—its solemn completion brings a sense of final gravity that the open-endedness of comedy struggles to obtain. Much the same could be said about how the death of moral and religious figures becomes central to our sense that they lived great lives, since they were capable of concluding them with the most sublime demonstration of their highest convictions. Socratès, Christ, Martin Luther King, Gandhi, Anne Frank, Mahsa Amini inspire by making their end recurse and reverberate back through the texture of their human existence.

Given its importance, it should therefore come as no surprise that Dworkin ascribes great value to the endeavor to die well. What makes his approach distinctive and profound is its rejection of a crude kind of hedonic utilitarianism which is so often the whipping boy of critics of euthanasia. In this reading, the primary argument for euthanasia is enabling individuals the chance to select avoiding pain they calculate

---

[17] See Ronald Dworkin. *Life's Dominion: An Argument About Abortion, Euthanasia, and Individual Freedom.* (New York, NY: Vintage Books, 1994) at pg 199.

[18] See Ronald Dworkin. *Life's Dominion: An Argument About Abortion, Euthanasia, and Individual Freedom.* (New York, NY: Vintage Books, 1994) at pg 199.

will outweigh whatever pleasure they may expect to experience if they continue to live. While this argument is of course important, it is vulnerable to the accusation that it reduces the value of human life to a purely subjective and instrumental conception. Life is only worth living to the extent it is pleasurable, or at least expected to be pleasurable overall. These kinds of positions have been very vulnerable to objections by many philosophers.[19] And of course they are extremely vulnerable to the objections of post-liberals and other religious groups, who can frame euthanasia as the grimly immanent endpoint of a philosophy for swine. R.R Reno even mocks "doctor-assisted suicide" and "euthanasia" as flowing from an "anti-metaphysical foundation" which holds that we should have total freedom over our body, which should not face "subjection to disease and decay."[20] Self-described "post-modern conservative" and post-liberal precursor Peter Lawler is even more emphatic when he describes euthanasia as appearing in a society that has lost a sense of caring, leading to a dystopian "embrace of euthanasia, a policy that is not death-accepting but death imposing...we would have reason to fear that [euthanasia] would be based not in caregiving love but care-denying utilitarianism, because the latter would be more characteristic of the excesses of the individual."[21]

For Dworkin, these conservative objections express an important pathos about the intrinsic value of life but miss how political acceptance of some forms of euthanasia is crucial to expressing that. Dworkin articulates three arguments for three different scenarios to this effect. The first is an argument from autonomy. He argues that since we agree that adults have a right to autonomy, which in turn has a deep relationship to integrity. Dworkin argues that having the right to choose to die protects "the capacity to express one's own character-values, commitment, convictions, and critical as well as experiential interests." This persists even in the event that one loses autonomy, for instance by becoming comatose, but expressed a wish to die in such circumstances.[22] Autonomy is a relatively

---

[19] Including others within the liberal and libertarian traditions such as Robert Nozick.

[20] See R.R Reno. *Resurrecting The Idea of a Christian Nation.* (New York, NY: Regenry Faith, 2016) at pg 19.

[21] See Peter Lawler. *Stuck with Virtue: The American Individual and Our Biotechnological Future.* (Wilmington, DE: ISI Books, 2005) at pg 150.

[22] See Ronald Dworkin. *Life's Dominion: An Argument About Abortion, Euthanasia, and Individual Freedom.* (New York, NY: Vintage Books, 1994) at pg 224.

easy case since it entails respecting the express choices made by adults concerning their interests. The other two are considerably more complex.

Secondly, there is an argument for beneficence which emerges when one person is entrusted to the care of another who is required to make decisions in the former's best interests. These become especially important when the beneficiary is not in an autonomous condition to decide for themselves whether it is in their interest for life to end, and left no indication of their considered preferences. In such circumstances Dworkin recommends the trustee's doubtless painful choices about their beneficiaries "experiential" interests should often take precedent, though here he is more taciturn about the need to reflect on the specificities of the relationship.[23]

Finally, Dworkin argues that people who suffering from debilitating and permanent mental conditions like dementia have a "right not to suffer indignity, not to be treated in ways that in their culture or community are understood as showing disrespect."[24] Framed in a different way, Dworkin argues that treating someone with dignity entails recognizing him "as a full human being, as someone whose fate we continue to treat as a matter of concern."[25] While he doesn't go so far as to argue that a decision to end life can be justified in terms of dignity, connecting the argument about dignity to the claims about autonomy and beneficence are suggestive. Since recognize that the manner of a person's death impacts the sense of their life as a whole, we can recognize their interest in not having that life polluted by dying in a profoundly undignified manner when a painful alternative is available. This would naturally be a very challenging case, since any decision to prematurely end life risks treating it is "not a matter of concern." But, as with beneficence, there may well be circumstances which emerge where we think a person's dignity would be so impugned by the measures needed to ensure their survival that death may be preferable. A person who expressed deep disdain at the prospect of bare life in a vegetal state, or a religious person who is profoundly opposed to blood transfusions, come to mind.

---

[23] See Ronald Dworkin. *Life's Dominion: An Argument About Abortion, Euthanasia, and Individual Freedom.* (New York, NY: Vintage Books, 1994) at pgs 229–233.

[24] See Ronald Dworkin. *Life's Dominion: An Argument About Abortion, Euthanasia, and Individual Freedom.* (New York, NY: Vintage Books, 1994) at pg 233.

[25] See Ronald Dworkin. *Life's Dominion: An Argument About Abortion, Euthanasia, and Individual Freedom.* (New York, NY: Vintage Books, 1994) at pg 236.

A Gentle Rejoinder to Dworkin on Abortion

Dworkin's arguments about abortion and euthanasia are invaluable in thinking through a liberal approach which doesn't reduce itself down to utilitarian calculus. While he is often at his poetic best when discussing euthanasia, without a doubt it is abortion which is currently and likely to remain the more dominant jurisprudential and political issue. Here we will briefly discuss some minor problems with Dworkin's approach to abortion, foregrounding its lack of deep engagement with radical feminist concerns. We will also discuss the problems with trying to side-step the question of metaphysical "personhood" or "selfhood" in the abortion debate by locating the germ of the debate in the question of constitutional personhood and fetal rights. Nevertheless, we conclude that Dworkin has a lot to offer liberals and progressives in a post-*Dobbs* climate.

Firstly, there is a meta-theoretical critique on can make about Dworkin's framing of the abortion issue. Dworkin's treatment of abortion largely conceives it purely as a "moral" issue that should be left to individual choice given its religious/spiritual significance. In this respect Dworkin frames abortion in methodologically and normatively individualist terms. While few feminists would disagree with Dworkin's normative individualist argument for a woman's right to choose, there is a sense in which presenting in which framing abortion in methodologically individualist terms is unduly myopic and even modestly masculist. It risks missing the broader picture of how restrictions on abortion are part and parcel of more encompassing forms of patriarchal domination.

For instance feminist materialists have often stressed how debates about restricting women's reproductive freedom are inevitably tied to the role they play in the social reproduction of society and the workforce. This in turn contributes to a "division of labor between the sexes, not only in child care but also in other activities of a broader scope."[26] Feminist materialist also highlight how this gendered ideology of women as defined by on child-rearing and caring forms of labor, and the concurrent diminishing emphasis on reproductive autonomy as central to women's well-being, instantiates itself in a vast number of ways. Given this, we can see why Dworkin's methodological individualism is not harmless. By

---

[26] See Kathryn Russell. "A Value-Theoretic Approach to Childbirth" in Rosemary Hennessy and Chrys Ingraham. *Materialist Feminist: A Reader in Class, Difference, and Women's Lives.* (New York, NY: Routledge Press, 1997) at pg 331.

focusing on this level it blunts our capacity to interrogate and understand the alignment of anti-abortion activism with broader patriarchal ideologies and laws. For instance, to ask why a Supreme Court Justice like Samuel Alito can callously argue that there is no long-standing right to abortion present in the "ordered liberty" traditions of the United States, ignoring how these were mainly the creation of well-heeled men who unwittingly relied on the labor of women living under conditions of patriarchal domination.[27]

Secondly, there is a sense in which Dworkin is too confident that the moral question about the moral legitimacy of choosing abortion can be cleanly segregated from metaphysical questions of personhood. Dworkin is surely right that all but the most fundamentalist accept that there is a meaningful ontological difference between a week old fertilized embryo and a birthed human child. He is also right that any sophisticated prochoice activist would have to admit that the embryo is "alive" and human in the genetic sense.

But it seems too quick to assume that since there is widespread agreement on these points, all that we are really deliberating is how best to show respect for the intrinsic value of human life and that this should be left for individuals to determine for themselves. This is part of what raises the temperature of the discussion for anti-abortion activists. Anyone convinced that an embryo is a full human person is unlikely to be persuaded by Dworkin's calm insistence that it is a question "simply too ambiguous to be useful" and that we should instead leave moral questions of when a human creature acquires interests and rights for itself, and when it embodies intrinsic value to individuals.[28]

This is because it truly matters for the debate whether the embryo is a collection of human cells with no subjective interest in perpetuating their existence, or a person who does have a subjective interest in perpetuating her existence which warrants moral respect. To put it analytically, we must carefully demarcate between biological human life and phenomenological human personhood. Very few of us would hold that the bare life of human tissue is in and of itself of moral worth, and consequently that haircuts or removing nails is a way of diminishing life, because we recognize that this

---

[27] See Catherine MacKinnon. *Towards a Feminist Theory of the State.* (Cambridge, MA: Harvard University Press, 1989).

[28] See Ronald Dworkin. *Life's Dominion: An Argument About Abortion, Euthanasia, and Individual Freedom.* (New York, NY: Vintage Books, 1994) at pg 22.

living human tissue doesn't bear on the personhood of the individual in question. In other words it does not seem so easy to demarcate either a "detached" or "derivative" argument for protecting human life from the metaphysical question of whether they are a person. If an embryo is not a person, but simply a collection of cells akin to other forms of disposable human tissue, then quite literally no one is harmed by its destruction. If an embryo is a person then she is harmed by the decision to destroy her, even if one might accept that a woman is entitled to do so to preserve her bodily autonomy.[29]

What's odd is that the metaphysical question of phenomenological human personhood is one which Dworkin should be receptive to, given his abiding interest in Gadamerian hermeneutics and the moral question of a persons "sense" of their complete life. What seems to be the most compelling argument against the claim that a fetus can be "harmed" is the fact that it lacks any phenomenological intentionalism toward either lifeworld world or biological existence which is a foundational characteristic of conscious personhood. In Heideggerian language, the fetus is not a phenomenological being because it lacks the "structural primordiality of care" which invests it in a past, present, and future and so gives moral meaning to its life. At least up to that dreaded "ambiguous" threshold where a fetus does transition into a person which cares in this way.

This is not the place for a complete discussion of these issues, so we will leave the objection at this. There do not seem to be good ontological arguments for the personhood of a fetus. This reinforces Dworkin's overall argument that decisions about abortion should be left to the individual's conscience up to a reasonable threshold where we can say a fetus comes to "care" about its lifeworld and existence to the extent of taking an intentional stance toward it. Even beyond that there are good Thomsonian arguments for respecting a woman's right to choose. Now we must move on from these metaphysical questions to the more political issues of what Dworkin has to offer liberals in a post-*Dobbs* context.

---

[29] See Judis Jarvis Thomson. "A Defense of Abortion." *Philosophy and Public Affairs*, Vol 1, No 1.

READING *DOBBS* THROUGH DWORKIN I

The *Dobbs* decision, while issued in 2022, is really the dark fruit of five decades of conservative activism. If the consequences weren't so transparently dire, there would be something admirable in the tenacity and drive behind it.[30] Indeed the *Dobbs* decision almost singularly displays the extent to which any understanding of American jurisprudence must take very seriously the dynamics of power and influence which surround the courts. The agonistic odyssey running from back alley abortions, to *Roe,* to the centrality of pro-life activism in right-wing circles, through the failure of *Casey,* to the scandals around Merrick Garland, Brett Kavanaugh, and Amy Comey Barrett looks set to fade into the background of the new status quo. It shouldn't. Any comprehensive response to the post-*Dobbs* reality will require far more than a cleverer set of jurisprudential arguments. Nevertheless the latter can't hurt, which is why it is useful to think of how Dworkinean arguments can contribute to the agitation to restore women's basic human rights.

There are several core issues raised by *Dobbs*. Two major ones concern us here.

The first concerns whether the American constitution includes a right to abortion. Adopting a narrowly originalist reading of the constitution which focuses on "the language of the instrument" Alito insists that on the surface of the text it clearly does not.

> The Constitution makes no express reference to a right to obtain an abortion, and therefore those who claim that it protects such a right must show that the right is somehow implicit in the constitutional text. Roe, however, was remarkably loose in its treatment of the constitutional text. It held that the abortion right, which is not mentioned in the Constitution, is part of a right to privacy, which is also not mentioned. See 410 U. S., at 152–153. And that privacy right, Roe observed, had been found to spring from no fewer than five different constitutional provisions—the First, Fourth, Fifth, Ninth, and Fourteenth Amendments.[31]

Nowhere is there an explicit right to abortion provisioned by the American constitution. Indeed, echoing the language of *Bowers v Hardwick,*

---

[30] See Obery Hendricks. *Christians Against Christianity: How Right-Wing Evangelicals Are Destroying Our Nation and Our Faith.* (Boston, MA: Beacon Press, 2021).

[31] See *Dobbs v. Jackson Women's Health Organization,* No. 19-1392, 597 U.S at pg 9.

Alito stresses how for much of American history the opposition presupposition was the case. "Until the latter part of the twentieth century, there was no support in American law for a constitutional right to obtain an abortion. No state constitutional provision had recognized such a right. Until a few years before Roe was handed down, no federal or state court had recognized such a right. Nor had any scholarly treatise of which we are aware."[32] For Alito, this primae facie legal and historical lack of an explicit right to an abortion—indeed not "only was there no support for such a constitutional right until shortly before *Roe*, but abortion had long been a crime in every single State."[33] So was sitting on a bus if you were a person of color, but go figure.

This leads to the second core claim. Discussing the precedents set by *Roe* and *Casey,* Justice Alito highlights how pro-choice activists have claimed the right to abortion is "implicitly protected" by other constitutional provisions.[34] Particularly those leaned on to develop the "right to privacy" many Americans consider of paramount importance, such as the First, Fourth, Fifth, Ninth, and Fourteenth Amendments. Of particular importance is an interpretation of the Fourteenth Amendment due process clause, which many argue protects "substantive" as well as procedural liberties. Including the liberty to have an abortion. But Alito is deeply wary of such claims, even leaning on some sarcastic language more associated with his deceased colleague Antonin Scalia. Proceeding with some caution, Alito accepts that there are some rights implicitly guaranteed by the constitution which are not explicitly enumerated. But, again leaning on very *Bowers*-like language, Alito draws on the tradition of "ordered liberty" conservatism to insist that any implicit right must be "deeply rooted in this Nation's history and tradition."[35] After a scholastic race through an almost exclusively male list of legal authors and sources, Alito reaches the apparently "inescapable conclusion is that a right to abortion is not deeply rooted in the Nation's history and traditions. On the contrary, an unbroken tradition of prohibiting abortion on pain of criminal punishment persisted from the earliest days of the common law

---

[32] See *Dobbs v. Jackson Women's Health Organization*, No. 19-1392, 597 U.S at pg 15.
[33] See *Dobbs v. Jackson Women's Health Organization*, No. 19-1392, 597 U.S at pg 16.
[34] See *Dobbs v. Jackson Women's Health Organization*, No. 19-1392, 597 U.S at pg 5.
[35] See *Dobbs v. Jackson Women's Health Organization*, No. 19-1392, 597 U.S at pg 5.

until 1973."[36] The last 50 years and majority support notwithstanding of course.

Interestingly, Alito seems aware that his sweeping indictment of 50 years of jurisprudence—apparently not enough to count as "deeply rooted" despite the fact that women have only been able to viably raise these concerns within that timeframe—raises major red flags beyond just the abortion issues. This is where he qualifies the mishmashed formalism and historicism of his early decision with an equally strange but no less strategic set of appeals to democratic localism and outright. On the one hand Alito insists that his decision does not forbid abortion, but merely restores the pre-*Roe* status quo where it is left to the people of the individual states to determine what they regard as appropriate. He insists that "the people of the various States may evaluate those interests differently. In some States, voters may believe that the abortion right should be even more extensive than the right that Roe and Casey recognized. Voters in other States may wish to impose tight restrictions based on their belief that abortion destroys an 'unborn human being.' Miss. Code Ann. §41–41–191(4)(b). Our Nation's historical understanding of ordered liberty does not prevent the people's elected representatives from deciding how abortion should be regulated."[37] But this appeal to a kind of demotic historicist relativism is undercut by Alito's decision to engage in moral metaphysics, describing the fetus in teleological terms which undercuts the libertarian appeal of abortion rights.

> What sharply distinguishes the abortion right from the rights recognized in the cases on which Roe and Casey rely is something that both those decisions acknowledged: Abortion destroys what those decisions call "potential life" and what the law at issue in this case regards as the life of an "unborn human being."[38]

---

[36] See *Dobbs v. Jackson Women's Health Organization*, No. 19-1392, 597 U.S at pg 25.

[37] See *Dobbs v. Jackson Women's Health Organization*, No. 19-1392, 597 U.S at pg 31.

[38] See *Dobbs v. Jackson Women's Health Organization*, No. 19-1392, 597 U.S at pg 32.

Reading *Dobbs* Through Dworkin II

For half a century, Roe v. Wade, 410 U. S. 113 (1973), and Planned Parenthood of Southeastern Pa. v. Casey, 505 U. S. 833 (1992), have protected the liberty and equality of women. Roe held, and Casey reaffirmed, that the Constitution safeguards a woman's right to decide for herself whether to bear a child. Roe held, and Casey reaffirmed, that in the first stages of pregnancy, the government could not make that choice for women. The government could not control a woman's body or the course of a woman's life: It could not determine what the woman's future would be. See Casey, 505 U. S., at 853; Gonzales v. Carhart, 550 U. S. 124, 171–172 (2007) (Ginsburg, J., dissenting). Respecting a woman as an autonomous being, and granting her full equality, meant giving her substantial choice over this most personal and most consequential of all life decisions.

Justice Breyer, Justice Sotomayor, and Justice Kagan in *Dobbs* v *Jackson*

The effect of this pretzeled set of argumentative appeals is to covey a very constipated kind of unprincipled reasoning which affirms the most militant criticisms of ordered liberty conservatism as basically an ostentatious species of irrationalism.[39] There is little else that can be said about an argument which moves from textuality formalism to ordered liberty conservatism, to demotic relativism, and then finally to third hand Aristotelianism-a mess of judgment that can only ever serve a model of sophism of a rarefied degree. This applies right down to Alito's fig leaf insistence that the *Dobbs* decision needn't be red as a green light to apply similar reasoning to other "implicit" rights read out the Fourteenth Amendment since the "exercise of the rights at issue in *Griswold, Eisenstadt, Lawrence,* and *Obergefell* does not destroy a 'potential life,' but an abortion has that effect."[40] Say whatever you will about him, but at least Clarence Thomas cares enough about the logic of malice to insist that "in future cases, we should reconsider all of this Court's substantive due

---

[39] For Dworkin's early critique of ordered liberty conservatism see Ronald Dworkin. "Lord Devlin and the Enforcement of Morals" *The Yale Law Journal*, Vol 75, No 6, 1966.

[40] See *Dobbs v. Jackson Women's Health Organization*, No. 19-1392, 597 U.S at pg 38.

process precedents, including *Griswold, Lawrence,* and *Obergefell"* in light of the precedent set in *Dobbs.*[41]

Interestingly, Dworkin wouldn't deny Alito's claim that a fetus constitutes a "potential" human life-though as we've argued his own reasoning on the questions of life and personhood could be fine tuned. Nor would he deny that historically American law has leaned toward the criminalization of abortion, reflecting citizens' long-standing concern to show respect for the intrinsic value of life. But Dworkin would emphatically reject Alito's bizarre pastiche of textualist and ordered liberty claims for their lack of principled integrity. Dworkin also denies that the fetus is entitled to constitutional protections of its interests; indeed, he'd highlight that nowhere does the American constitution indicate that the law must show concern for the interests or rights of unborn "potential" life over and against the liberties of individual citizens. Consequently Alito's decision to grant "unborn" life such normative weight is itself extra-textualist, and nowhere justified as a matter of principle.

This means that in fact Alito's argument relies exclusively on its frothy blend of ordered liberty conservatism and demotic relativism as a principled argument for erasing rights to abortion and turning such matters over to the states. But Dworkin would reject this by insisting that turning private matters of conscience—which Alito concedes are debatable and multi-faceted—over to state legislatures is deeply unprincipled. To add a feminist flourish to his typical argumentation, this is because through denying women the liberty to make decisions about their own reproductive destiny the law fails to show them the equal respect that is foundational to legitimating the American system of government. Moreover, we can add to this that this in turn impoverishes Alito's conception of democracy by reducing it to a kind of crude demotic relativism, wherein state legislatures—many themselves skewed by gerrymandering—are allowed to decide on these issues of conscience. But this entails denying equal democratic partnership to cis-women and trans-men capable of reproduction, by subordinating their right to decide profoundly private issues of conscience to transient majoritarianism. In brief, Alito has everything backwards. It is precisely because abortion is contentious and impactful that it should not be left to state legislatures to

---

[41] See *Dobbs v. Jackson Women's Health Organization,* No. 19-1392, 597 U.S at pg 3.

decide, but instead those individuals who are most effected by the decision to carry a fetus to term or not. Failing to do so means the law fails to show equal concern for the dignity and life-plans of millions of women who, as the dissent powerfully noted, "have today lost a fundamental constitutional protection—."[42]

CONCLUSION

Dworkin's treatment of abortion and euthanasia demonstrates the subtle but key different between moral seriousness and moral fundamentalism. Moral seriousness doesn't run from hard problems any more than a jurist runs from hard cases, but instead respects how the gravity of the problem at hand will bear on her own integrity and that of her community. It recognizes how addressing moral problems requires the deepest reflection on our core convictions, in this case on life and its value, without following into the nihilism of external skepticism or the impotence of internal skepticism. This is the exacting task which to which all of us are called, but sadly few of us answer. Moral fundamentalism, on the other hand, is the opposite of seriousness. It does not respect the gravity of the problems at hand and confront them. Moral fundamentalism retreats into the solipsistic yearning for certainty on the cheap which is the affective basis of all ruling ideologies, whether they instantiate patriarchy or economic domination. The price is high, since the lack of integrity characteristic of moral fundamentalism means its alleged virtues are inauthentic and polluted. In the individual, the yearning for certainty subordinates all integral striving for truth about value. Socially this is expressed not as principled confidence. Instead one sees the anxious fear that unless others are compelled to live by our cheap certainties they will become exposed as the heteronomy they are. And so, countless pleasing illusions are forced upon us to tranquilize the existential dread of the easily frightened and self-imposed immaturity remains the law of the land.

We say this in a context where the Supreme Court of the United States has stripped millions of women of a right their parents and grandparents enjoyed, motivated by no little nostalgia for an era where fundamentalism

---

[42] See Breyer, Sotomayor, and Kagan, J.J., dissenting in *Dobbs v. Jackson Women's Health Organization*, No. 19-1392, 597 U.S at pg 60.

can mark itself as moral seriousness without being called out. It is uncertain what the future holds for abortion and euthanasia rights in a political climate where the citizenry is remaining or becoming more liberal while its court becomes more aloof. But it is clear that this debate isn't over.

CHAPTER 6

Equal Opportunity and the Burden of Student Debt

Abstract This chapter discusses Dworkin's liberal egalitarian arguments for "equality of resources" and makes the case for its relevance in an era of increasing inequality. Avoiding the technical jargon often present in discussions of distributive justice, the chapter makes the political theoretical claim that equality of resources would be central to realizing the American dream of everyone having a fair start in life. The chapter concludes with a discussion of recent debates on student debt relief and educational access.

THE AMERICAN DREAM

At the center of the American Dream—the promise that "anyone, regardless of his or her origins, can have a fair start in life. If we work hard, we can get a good education and achieve success"[1]—is the commitment to equal opportunities for all citizens. In practice, any consensus around the American Dream is misleading because there is no uniform understanding of what equality of opportunity means or requires from our legal and political institutions. For most Americans, equality of opportunity amounts to recognition that people are in their everyday lives

---

[1] Robert Putnam. *Our Kids: The American Dream in Crisis.* (New York: Simon & Schuster, 2015), cover notes.

© The Author(s), under exclusive license to Springer Nature
Switzerland AG 2023
L. A. Jacobs and M. McManus, *Against Post-Liberal Courts and Justice*,
Palgrave Studies in Classical Liberalism,
https://doi.org/10.1007/978-3-031-45347-2_6

in competitive races to succeed as measured by income, wealth, jobs, school, and social status. Of course, not everyone wins in these races; there are always winners and losers in competitions for success. That principle requires more than a set of formal rules to prevent the exclusion of individuals from achieving success in these races by making reference to personal characteristics that are arbitrary, such as race, socio-economic class, gender, religion, and sexuality. What genuine equality of opportunity requires is that the races themselves be in some sense fair—that everyone, regardless of race, wealth, socio-economic class, gender, religion, or sexuality, has the opportunity to compete and the possibility to be successful.

In the United States, the President and Congress have for a century played an important role in promoting this sort of ideal of equal opportunities for all. The courts have had a much more limited role in advancing equality of opportunity, especially with regard to economic inequality and class differences. Indeed, there is considerable evidence that the US Supreme Court has for fifty years significantly hindered greater economic equality among American citizens, even if they have supported equality of opportunity.[2] But we suggest in this chapter that a post-liberal Supreme Court has begun to issue decisions that reject the very ideal of equality of opportunity for all American citizens.

What can be expected from a post-liberal justice system is that it hinders initiatives by the President or Congress that advance equality of opportunity, especially ones that redistribute wealth from wealthy Americans to the disadvantaged. The concrete illustration of this is the recent judicial review by the Supreme Court of the Biden administration's initiative to cancel a significant amount of student debt for 43 million Americans. Student debt has been growing at an alarming rate, a reflection of the increasing cost of post-secondary education. This debt has proven to be a major hindrance for many people in their pursuit of the American Dream, in effect, stifling their opportunities for success. In 2023, the Supreme Court, by a majority of 6–3, ruled in *Biden v. Nebraska* that any initiative to cancel student debt in a comprehensive manner is so costly to taxpayers that it was outside the authority of the executive branch and can only be an initiative coming from Congress.

---

[2] Adam Cohen. *Supreme Inequality: The Supreme Court's Fifty Year Battle for a More Unjust America.* (New York: Penguin Books, 2020).

FAIRNESS AND EQUALITY OF OPPORTUNITY

At the core of equality of opportunity is the concept that in competitive procedures such as labor markets and wealth accumulation designed for the allocation of scarce resources and the distribution of the benefits and burdens of social life, these procedures should be governed by criteria that are relevant to the particular goods at stake in the competition and not by irrelevant considerations such as race, religion, class, gender, disability, sexual orientation, ethnicity, or other factors that may hinder some of the competitors' prospects for success. In this sense, equality of opportunity is an ideal for the fair regulation of competitions that distribute valuable opportunities that constitute the American Dream.[3]

It is possible to distinguish three dimensions of fairness that might guide the fair regulation of competitions. *Procedural fairness* stems from a concern with the basic rules of procedure that guide a competition including the determination of the winners. *Background fairness* stems from a concern that there is a level playing field for all competitors. *Stakes fairness* stems from a concern with the size or nature of the prizes or what is at stake in the competition. This third kind of fairness plays an innovative role in an account of equality of opportunity because of its capacity to constrain the risky pursuit of equal opportunities for all.

These three dimensions of equality of opportunity can be illustrated by considering the example of a boxing match. Boxing matches characteristically are regulated by certain familiar rules—the so-called Queensberry Rules. Some of these rules reflect *procedural fairness* such as, for instance, not punching one's opponent below the waist, no head butting, no swinging after the bell goes to end the round, and so on. Likewise, fair matches do not begin with an agreed-upon winner; instead, the winner is determined by the rules such as who wins by a knock-out or scores the most points in the case of a decision fight. Considerations of procedural fairness in this sense are presumably quite familiar. But boxing matches typically respect another dimension of fairness, as well. In competitions such as the Olympics, boxers are classified based on their body weight and fight other boxers in the same class. Underlying this practice is the intuition that there is something fundamentally unfair about a match between a 125 pound featherweight boxer and a 200 pound heavyweight.

---

[3] See Lesley Jacobs. *Pursuing Equal Opportunities*. (New York, NY: Cambridge University Press, 2004), ch. 1.

Assuming that the heavy weight boxer wins a match between the two, that outcome is said to be unfair even if the boxer did not violate the rules of procedural fairness such as hitting the featherweight boxer after the bell ended the round. *Background fairness* reflects the concern that boxers enter a match on roughly equal terms with respect to body weight. Background fairness is met, in other words, when there is a level playing field for all competitors. The third dimension of fairness concerns the prizes, how the winner is determined, or what is at stake in the boxing match. The idea that the winner in a boxing match is determined by a knock-out or points (as opposed to say fighting until death) is part of this dimension. In for instance professional boxing, the stake prize is money and a title. The practice is to have the winner receive say 75% of the money (say $750,000) and the loser 25% (250,000). The justification typically is that this is fairer than a winner-take-all prize of $1,000,000. The dimension of fairness drawn upon here is what is meant by *stakes fairness*.[4]

What standards underlie these three dimensions of fairness? The standards of procedural fairness are generally specific to the particular competition. What counts as procedurally fair is often linked to what is at stake in the competition or is intended to protect participants from certain risks. In many competitions, the basic requirements of procedural fairness are not deeply contested. Those requirements often reflect a general consensus and have developed over time. Sometimes, of course, the rules or regulations governing a competition are found to be unfair and to violate procedural fairness. The clearest breaches of procedural fairness involve the exclusion of certain classes of persons from the competition. There are well known historical examples of this in professions such as law, medicine, and teaching.

Stakes fairness reflects a concern with the distribution of benefits and burdens within a competition and what constitutes winning or losing. Part of the issue here is concerns whether it is fair to have, for instance, a winner-take-all scheme. Imagine, say, divorce settlements that were structured in this way. Most of us would object that this is unfair because it is wrong to have the stakes so high; while it may be acceptable to have the winner receive more benefits, it is unfair that the loser receives nothing. Similarly, consider the labor market in this light. Often, employment in the competitive labor market is perceived in this way; those who get jobs

---

[4] See especially Lesley Jacobs. "Equality, Adequacy, and Stakes Fairness", *Theory and Research in Education*, Vol 8, 2010, 249–268.

receive wages and all other sorts of fringe benefits. One way to view a range of government program from unemployment insurance to workfare is as mechanisms to promote stakes fairness rather than attaching all the benefits to the winners in the competitive labor market.

Background fairness has become the most familiar site for equal opportunities concerns about fair competition. This dimension of fairness fixates on the initial starting positions or backgrounds of those potentially involved in a competition. The underlying insight is, of course, that the structure of these positions will affect who competes and how they will fare in the competition. From the perspective of competitive equality of opportunity, because pre-existing inequalities infect the fairness of competitive processes, there is a need to regulate these processes with a sensitivity to remedies for these inequalities. Ronald Dworkin offers, one particularly compelling account of background fairness, which he calls Equality of Resources.

EQUALITY OF RESOURCES

At the center of Dworkin's theory of equality of resources is the distinction between a person's choices and their circumstances. A person's choices are their own unique personal responsibility.[5] They make those choices and they should expect to live with the consequences, good or bad. Someone's circumstances include their material resources, talents, and skills, as mental and physical capabilities. Fairness demands that two principles operate in concert:

> The first principle requires government to adopt laws and policies that insure that its citizens' fates are, so far as government can achieve this, insensitive to who they otherwise are – their economic background, gender, race, or particular set of skills and handicaps. The second principle demands that government work, again so far as it can achieve this, to make their fates sensitive to the choices they have made.[6]

[5] Ronald Dworkin. *Justice for Hedgehogs*. (Cambridge, MA: Harvard University Press, 2011), chs. 9–10.

[6] Ronald Dworkin. *Sovereign Virtue*. (Cambridge, MA: Harvard University Press, 2000), p. 6.

To put it in other terms, in Dworkin's view, because circumstances should be choice insensitive, background fairness holds when no economic transfer would make one person's circumstances more equal to the circumstances of anyone else.

A basic axiom of Dworkin's position is this: equality of resources is concerned fundamentally with the share of resources devoted to the whole life of an individual. People are treated fairly when their share of resources across their lives as a whole is equal. This requires that any government scheme that distributes resources such as money, debt relief, or even health care be sensitive to the cost of each person's life to other people. That cost is measured by how valuable the resources and other elements of circumstances used by that person are to those other people. Dworkin calls this cost the opportunity cost of one's life. He recognizes that people will choose to do different things in the initial circumstances they are born into. One person might prefer to work hard and produce more resources; someone else may only consume the resources they received. Some people may nourish and develop their innate skills and talents; others may choose not to. Inevitably, some people will over time accumulate more wealth and resources than others because of the choices they make. But this does not mean that the inequality is unfair. Provided that each is equal in terms of the circumstances devoted to the whole of their lives, differences traceable to personal responsibility are still consistent with equality of opportunity. It is in this sense that equality of resources is in Dworkin's terms choice-sensitive or ambition-sensitive.[7]

What is the best way to measure opportunity costs? For Dworkin, this role is assigned to the economic market for goods. Imagine, he suggests, the situation of a group of shipwrecked survivors washed up on a desert island with an abundance of resources. The issue is how to distribute fairly those resources that are to be privately owned. Some form of auction or market is proposed. One basic requirement is that all of the shipwrecked immigrants enter the market on equal terms, which requires that everyone has the same number of counters or tokens to be used for bidding in the auction. The initial challenge is to propose a set of prices at which each of the resources will be sold. The person who has this task must post a set of prices that "clear the market," meaning that only one person among the bidders is willing to pay for the price for each resource and that

---

[7] Dworkin. *Sovereign Virtue*, ch. 2.

all the resources on the island are sold. The importance of price-setting in this way is that it determines how valuable each resource is to other people, or in other ways, a way to measure opportunity costs. Of course, if one is the buyer of a resource at the price of x tokens, this means that they have fewer tokens to buy other resources. The consequent bundle of resources each person has after the successful running of the auction where everyone has spent all of their tokens constitutes a fair share of the island's resources.

After the initial auction, the markets will stay open, allowing people to buy and sell the resources they have acquired. Recall however that a person's circumstances include more than the resources they have; it also includes the talents and skills they are born with and other types of physical and mental endowments. The problem on the desert island is that because talents and endowments cannot be transferred among persons, they cannot be bid for in the auction like the more commodifiable resources. Dworkin's innovative solution to this problem is to have operating alongside the economic market for transferable goods and resources, a progressive income tax scheme modeled on a hypothetical insurance market, in which people pay a premium to insure that they are compensated when they lack the particular talents and skills they themselves value. This insurance market is a complex way to make sure that inequalities resulting from differences in talents and skills—differences in circumstances—are themselves choice-sensitive.

Educational Opportunities as Ladders to Success

At the core of the American Dream and equality of opportunity today is the belief that education provides ladders of opportunity and enables upward mobility for socially disadvantaged students. Education functions as the great equalizer that enables Americans to enter into competitions for societal goods like good jobs and greater wealth. Ron Haskins and Isabel Sawhill recently explained,

> America has long been viewed as the land of opportunity, a country in which everyone has the chance to work hard and get ahead. Hard work may have been enough in the past, but several developments...have added a new subtext to the story of opportunity in America. Good jobs are now usually based on knowledge and skills. This development, in turn, has made education and training the motor of both economic mobility and

the American economy. For most Americans the path to economic success lies through the schoolhouse door.[8]

The fundamental insight is that fair access to education is the foundation to realizing the American Dream.

The insight itself traces back to the civil rights era of the 1950s and 1960s. In a famous report that had it origins in the 1964 Civil Rights Act, James Coleman wrote,

> In the first century of this Nation's history, opportunity was associated with the frontier...For much of the second century opportunity has been associated with expanding industrial enterprise...Today, opportunity must be found in a highly organized technological society; the scientist is the symbol of success. Public schools are the principal means in our society for providing opportunity by developing mental skills and imparting knowledge...necessary for further education and for today's occupations...In this perspective, the question of this report becomes a simple one: How well do the schools of our Nation provide such opportunity for minority children who would otherwise begin adult life with a distinct disadvantage?[9]

The core vision of the importance of education mirrors the statement by Chief Justice Warren of the US Supreme Court in *Brown v. Board of Education of Topeka* a decade earlier:

> In these days, it is doubtful that any child may reasonably be expected to succeed in life if he is denied the opportunity of an education. Such an opportunity, where the state has undertaken to provide it, is a right which must be made available to all on equal terms.[10]

In both Coleman's Report and Chief Justice Warren's statement, the focus is on public schools. Despite immense differences in funding levels, public schools were then and are today free for all students.

---

[8] Ron Haskins and Isabel Sawhill. *Creating an Opportunity Society.* (Washington, DC: Brookings Institution Press, 2009), 125–126.

[9] James Coleman et al. *Equality of Educational Opportunity.* (Washington, DC: U.S. Government Printing Office, 1966), 36.

[10] Brown v. Board of Education of Topeka (1954) 347 US 490 @493.

Today, the focus for discussions of equality of opportunity has shifted from public schools to post-secondary education. College or university attendance is now a key ladder for upward social mobility and the advancement of equality of opportunity. Attending college or university is now seen as a requirement for most Americans to compete for higher incomes, greater wealth, and better jobs. Unlike public schools, attending college or university is not free. Students have to pay tuition and often living expenses if they are attending a college or university away from home. But the cost of going to college or university is special, as compared to say the cost of buying a new car, because it has become this ladder for opportunity and social mobility. Unfortunately, these costs have been escalating dramatically over the past three decades. An increasing number of students are borrowing money to attend college or university. In fact, total student debt in the United States has quadrupled since 2006—only mortgage debt is greater. It is estimated that 46 million Americans are carrying student loans. And there is compelling evidence that shows that student debt is constraining the opportunities of those Americans, affecting when and if they get married and have children, buy a home, and even the jobs they apply for.[11]

BIDEN V. NEBRASKA

During the COVID-19 pandemic, the Trump Administration and then the Biden Administration paused repayment of student loans—a measure that was immensely popular and indicated the bi-partisan consensus that student debt has become a drag on equality of opportunity for many Americans. Following through on an election promise during the 2020 campaign, President Biden initiated a comprehensive program to cancel some student debt for 43 million Americans without new legislation. The program proposed to cancel up to $10,000 for all student debt holders plus another $10,000 for student debt holders who were Pell grant recipients, meaning that they had been identified as students having exceptional financial need.

---

[11] Council on Foreign Relations. "Is Rising Student Debt Harming the U.S. Economy?" (October 20, 2022). https://www.cfr.org/backgrounder/us-student-loan-debt-trends-economic-impact?gclid=CjwKCAjw8symBhAqEiwAaTA__MDe9J6Cvz7jHunt UXeKohJfxNU2JTdeo-aUmgPHWeg274qaemkQchoCegkQAvD_BwE.

Is canceling student debt unfair? Is it inconsistent with equality of opportunity? Certainly for Dworkin this is a complex question to answer. Indeed, this example illustrates precisely the need to balance the principle of being concerned that each citizen's fate or life chances are not determined by their economic background, gender, or race, and the principle that government works to make those individuals' life chances sensitive to the choices they have made. As we have just highlighted, Dworkin maintained that personal responsibility is one of the two foundational principles underlying equality of resources. Some people made choices to take on debt in order to go to school where others in similar circumstances chose not to. And others who took on student debt made sacrifices—foregoing vacations or not buying a new car—after completing college or education to pay down their debt more quickly than others who were less willing to make such sacrifices. Recognizing the importance of personal responsibility necessitates paying attention to the fairness of who benefits. The strength of the special student debt relief the Biden Administration's program intended to provide to Pell Grant recipients is presumably a reflection of the fact that for those individuals taking on student debt was not in any sense a choice; their financial hardship was so significant that no amount of sacrifice would have enabled them to go to college or university without taking on some student debt.

Aside from concerns about giving personal responsibility its due, it is also fundamental to recognize that college or university attendance is constitutive of what genuine equality of opportunity and the pursuit of the American Dream means today. The increasing cost of post-secondary education combined with more people attending college or university has largely driven the student debt crisis. Providing relief for 43 million Americans with student debt is for the Biden Administration an investment in equality of opportunity, and support for their pursuit of the American Dream. Arguably, the Biden Administration's proposal was fair, on Dworkin's terms, because it was not the cancelation of all student debt—as some in the Democratic Party sought—but rather provided some limited relief for those burdened by student debt. The initiative would have canceled all of the student debt for 20 million individuals and reduced student debt for another 23 million people—98% of all Americans burdened by student debt. The estimated cost of the initiative was $430 billion in debt principal, roughly 25% of the total student debt owed by Americans.

The majority of the Supreme Court in their judicial review of the initiative do not directly engage in the fairness of the initiative. Instead, the initiative was struck down on the principal grounds that the Biden Administration—the Secretary of Education more specifically—did not have the authority to implement a program that benefited so many Americans: "The authority to 'modify' statutes and regulations allows the Secretary to make modest adjustments and additions to existing provisions, not transform them... From a few narrowly delineated situations specified by Congress, the Secretary has expanded forgiveness to nearly every borrower in the country."[12]

Chief Justice Roberts, writing for the majority, objects to what he sees as the radical character of the initiative: "What the Secretary has actually done is draft a new section of the Education Act from scratch by 'waiving' provisions root and branch and then filling the empty space with radically new text."[13] And in the same vein, "The Secretary's comprehensive debt cancellation plan cannot fairly be called a waiver—it not only nullifies existing provisions, but augments and expands them dramatically."[14] What precisely for the Chief Justice is so radical about the initiative? His answer: "the Secretary of Education claims the authority, on his own, to release 43 million borrowers from their obligations to repay $430 billion in student loans... The 'economic and political significance' of the Secretary's action is staggering by any measure and can unilaterally alter large sections of the American economy."[15]

The reasoning of Chief Justice Roberts in *Biden v. Nebraska* is clear but telling. In American society today, post-secondary education is a ladder to success and the opportunity to attend college or university is the bedrock of a national commitment to equal opportunities for all citizens, regardless of their economic or familial background. The student debt crisis has for this reason put pressure on the commitment to equality of opportunity. And serious measures to address that crisis are best viewed as taking equality of opportunity seriously. By framing the Biden Administration's student debt relief initiative as radical, Chief Justice Roberts has likely

---

[12] Biden v. Nebraska, 600 U. S. ___(2023) at 13–14.

[13] Biden v. Nebraska, 600 U. S. ___(2023) at 17.

[14] Biden v. Nebraska, 600 U. S. ___(2023) at 18.

[15] Biden v. Nebraska, 600 U. S. ___(2023) at 20 & 25.

revealed that a majority of justices on the US Supreme Court—for the first time in more than a century—no longer are committed to equality of opportunity and the American Dream for all citizens.

CONCLUSION

The prospects of post-liberal courts moving away from a foundational commitment to equality of opportunity are dire for so much that governments do in the social policy space. From health care to education to income support and veterans affairs, it is easy to imagine far-reaching court decisions that put aside substantive concerns about background fairness. At the same time, it must also be recognized that social policy tied to the so-called welfare state has proven to be surprisingly resilient.[16] This resilience is in part a reflection of the multiple purposes welfare state institutions serve. Universities and colleges are not only great equalizers to advance equality of opportunity; they are also a major source of talent for industry and the private sector. Likewise, not only does the health care system meet the diverse medical needs of so many Americans, it is also one of the largest employers in the country. Government income support schemes help indigent populations but are also a lifeline for small businesses. What we can expect to see, as post-liberal courts exercise judicial review that constrains these institutions, is innovation in achieving progressive objectives outside the scope of judicial review. Case in point is the response by the Biden Administration to the Supreme Court's decision in *Biden v. Nebraska*. Within weeks of the ruling, a new initiative was announced that provided student debt relief to 3.4 million borrowers with an estimated cost of $116 billion.

---

[16] Paul Pierson. *Dismantling the Welfare State*. (New York: Cambridge University Press, 1994).

CHAPTER 7

Reading Dworkin Against Post-Liberal Justice

Abstract This chapter concludes the book with a critical analysis of the emerging post-liberal approach to jurisprudence, as exemplified in the thinking of Patrick Deneen and Adrian Vermeule. We argue that post-liberalism constitutes a powerful rival to the liberal approach to justice and law, which requires liberalism reinvent itself on more egalitarian lines. The chapter and book conclude with a call for a more inspiring and inclusive liberal jurisprudence integrally committed to securing liberty, equality, and solidarity for all.

Keywords Post-liberalism · Common Good Constitutionalism · Adrian Vermeule · Patrick Deneen

WHAT IS POST-LIBERALISM?

The gradual conservative takeover of the courts prefaced a far more dramatic transition in the 2010s which no doubt would have horrified Dworkin as it did many of us. Starting with Hungary, the world saw

© The Author(s), under exclusive license to Springer Nature   105
Switzerland AG 2023
L. A. Jacobs and M. McManus, *Against Post-Liberal Courts and Justice*,
Palgrave Studies in Classical Liberalism,
https://doi.org/10.1007/978-3-031-45347-2_7

a wave of right-wing populists and self-described "illiberal democrats"[1] sweep to power. By 2018 the United States, Russia, Brazil, India, Italy, Poland, Hungary—almost every major state on earth—was impacted. While a combination of shifting electoral fortunes, ineptitude at handling the COVID pandemic and resultant economic misery, and progressive pushback stemmed the tide by 2020 it isn't clear whether we are simply in the eye of the hurricane.

Accompanying this political transition was a truly dizzying collection of books, op-eds, and online content that sought to make sense of the transition. While many of these were critical or every critical, a significant number of conservative intellectuals and movements expressed sympathy or even enthusiasm for the rise of the hard right. Far and away the most intellectually sophisticated were the "post-liberals"—a collection of mostly Catholic scholars who conceded the vulgarity of much of Trumpism and illiberal democracy, but defended it as either a predictable reaction to liberal extremism or a desirable transition to a new kind of socially conservative integralist state.

Post-liberalism has deep intellectual roots which have served it well in the culture wars of the twenty-first century. Unlike pulpier and angrier forms of Jordan Shapiroisms, post-liberals tend to be highly scholarly, bookish, and intellectually syncretic. Deeply indebted to conservative flavors of scholasticism, particularly Thomism, post-liberalism's clearest antecedents nonetheless lie in the often hostile Catholic response to Enlightenment modernity. Joseph De Maistre's venomous denunciation of the "Satanic" liberal revolutionaries, Cardinal Newman's nostalgic apologias for faith in an industrializing era, and G.K Chesterton's jocular defense of commonsensical orthodoxy cast a long shadow. More immediately Leo Strauss' critique of historicism and, the "post" modern conservatism of Peter Lawler, the natural-law jurisprudence of John Finnis, and Christopher Lasch's lamentations around cultural narcissism are all important influences. Though interestingly, some post-liberals are even open to borrowing from the left: Catherine Mackinnon's denunciation of pornography, Adorno's critique of the culture industry, and even

---

[1] Csaba Toth. "Full Text of Viktor Orbán's Speech at Băile Tuşnad (Tusnádfürdő) of 26 July 2014." *The Budapest Beacon*, July 29, 2014.

some echoes of the Marxist critique of political economy have made their way into the post-liberal's work.[2]

Patrick Deneen's *Why Liberalism Failed* is the most popular and systematic post-liberal work thus far. It reconstructs many of the classical objections of liberalism but articulates them in novel forms. For Deneen, liberalism didn't fail because of external enemies. By the end of the twentieth-century liberalism had vanquished fascism on the right and communism on the left, reigning supreme as the world's hegemonic ideology and announcing an "end" to history. Liberalism failed because it succeeded, brought low by immanent contradictions which served to discredit it. As he puts it:

> Liberalism's own successes makes it difficult to sustain reflection on the likelihood that the greatest current threat to liberalism lies not outside and beyond liberalism but within it. The potency of this threat arises from the fundamental nature of liberalism, from what they are thought to be its very strengths-especially its faith in its ability of self-correction and its belief in progress and continual improvement-which make it largely impervious to discerning its deepest weaknesses and even self-inflicted decline. No matter our contemporary malady, there is no challenge that can't be fixed by a more perfect application of liberal solutions.[3]

In Deneen's telling the real founder of liberalism was Francis Bacon, who dismissed the antiquarian natural-law tradition and held that human knowledge should be deployed to achieve power over nature and reorganize it to instrumentally service human needs. This married very well to Locke's atomized liberal anthropology, consisting of segregated individuals pursuing their self-interest with minimal regard for one another or interest in higher order concerns. Lockean individuals exercised their intelligence and labor to bring the world to heel, seeking to permanently emancipate themselves from any and all constraints. While this initially led liberals to demand constraints on power, in the long run liberals saw felt compelled to acquire and exercise power to liberate humanity from nature itself. Here liberal proponents of market and state solutions, far

---

[2] A split of sorts has occurred on this front, with the more "right" leaning post-liberals writing for the increasingly hard right *First Things* magazine while the "left" has gravitated to the experimental and irreverent *Compact*.

[3] See Patrick Deneen. *Why Liberalism Failed*. (New Haven, CN: Yale University Press, 2018) at pgs. 28–29.

from being radically opposed, are united in their basic conviction that the sole end of collective activity must be a never-ending Promethean ascent. They only differ on the best means to achieve that; and even there, not as much as one might think. The result has been the creation of highly alienated societies where each individual is thrown back on themselves, politically animated only by whichever form of liberal ideology offers them the most power. For the working class, this has resulted in lonely and tough existences relieved only by the partial gratification of petty appetites while a "new aristocracy" gets to engage in narcissistic Millsian "experiments in living. Custom has been routed: much of what today passes for culture—with or without the adjective 'popular'—consists of mocking sarcasm and irony..."[4] Given these conditions, Deneen holds that it should be no surprise that liberalism is everywhere failing. While he is wary of embracing Trumpism, Deneen ends his book with a call to preserving certain achievements of the liberal tradition while moving into a new post-liberal future.

Like most sophisticated critiques of liberalism, there is undoubtedly something to Deneen's post-liberal critique. The ideology of neoliberal possessive individualism has rolled back many of the post-War institutions, from unions to an expanding welfare state, which helped engender a sense of communitarian solidarity and reflected a commitment to the equal worth of all citizens. It is also the case that liberal intellectuals can be blamed for not doing enough to resist this decline and so contributing to the conditions which led to the emergence of an illiberal hard right. This includes Dworkin in some of his more elitist moments. Dworkin's tendency to lean very heavily on courts rather than democracy as the vehicle for liberal reform was at the very least dangerous and at worst misguided.

But it is also the case that, like most sophisticated critiques of liberalism, the cure offered by post-liberals can seem far worse than the disease. This will become clear when we look at the post-liberal approach to jurisprudence, which threatens a return to the worst forms of illiberal authoritarianism under the guise of promoting the "common good."

---

[4] Patrick Deneen. *Why Liberalism Failed.* (New Haven, CN: Yale University Press, 2018) at pg 146.

A Post-Liberal Jurisprudence

Schmitt and Francis, in their different registers, suggest the problem I want to identify and discuss here: the relentless dynamic of liberalism tends to undermine the "peace, security and order" that liberalism itself promises. What liberalism cannot obey are the natural principles or, if you like, natural laws of political rule that go under the label of *Ragion di Stato*, principles and laws that no ruler can forever defy without undermining the very conditions of his rule Minds more powerful than my own have argued that liberalism, in one way or another, undermines itself. The mechanisms proposed to this end are numerous and various. My project is to add one such mechanism, whose claim to consideration is that it captures the distinctive nature of *sacramental* liberalism—an essentially religious movement and set of commitments, with a distinctive soteriology, eschatology and ecclesiology. To the extent this mechanism has been overlooked, it is because earlier theorists were oblivious to the categories of constitutional and political theology, to the theological and liturgical dimensions of liberalism, and to Cardinal Manning's dictum: "all human conflict is ultimately theological."

Adrian Vermeule, "All Human Conflict Is Ultimately Theological"

Deneen is undoubtedly the most significant political philosopher and critic within the post-liberal movement. But it is in the Schmitt-inflected writings of Adrian Vermeule, the movement's chief jurist and homophobe, that we get a clearer vision of what a post-liberal jurisprudence and society would look like. And it is horrifying.

Vermeule is currently the Ralph S. Tyler Professor of Constitutional Law at Harvard University, and a growing influence on the American right more generally. Vermeule began his career as an accomplished analyst of the administrative state and the executive branch, before taking a sharp turn after his conversion to Roman Catholicism in 2016. Since then he has taken considerable glee in needling both legal liberals and more conventional legal conservatives. In particular his 2020 *Atlantic* essay "Beyond Originalism"—which held that originalism "has now outlived its utility, and has become an obstacle to the development of a robust, substantively conservative approach to constitutional law and interpretation..." provoked a flurry of outraged responses from many on his own team.[5] Not one to back down, Vermeule has gone a step further in his recent *Common Good Constitutionalism*, where he argues that in fact Dworkin's objections to originalism were entirely right and have "never been successfully answered" by proponents.[6] Vermeule relishes pointing out how all responses to Dworkin's and other similar objections, like Jack Balkin's "living originalism," effectively end up conceding everything critics of originalism could want. Far from being a "neutral" and judicially impartial way of interpreting the American constitution, originalism evolves into just another semantic fig leaf through which Judges articulate their political convictions.

Vermeule's rearticulation of Dworkinean objections to originalism echoes a familiar reactionary trope. As Corey Robin points out, the most creative conservative thinkers are typically those who are the best students of the left. They learn from its rhetoric, methods, and strategies and reinvent them to serve right-wing purposes.[7] Or as Edmund Neill puts it, they develop "symbiotic opposites to progressive concepts in order to rebut them."[8] The "common good constitutionalism" advocated for by Vermeule very much falls into this paradigm. Appropriating Dworkin's arguments about the irrevocably philosophical and moral dimensions of legal interpretation, he argues that conservative jurists are naïve in thinking that legal officials can just impartially dole out the law. Indeed, Vermeule points out how even adopting such a standpoint echoes antiquarian classical liberal and positivist myths about the need for legal impartiality and neutrality. Once this is abandoned, conservatives can develop a "common good constitutionalism" which, "although not enslaved to the original meaning of the constitution, also rejects the progressive overarching sacramental narrative, the relentless expansion of individualistic autonomy."[9] By contrast common good constitutionalism can be defined in terms of the "classical law" tradition:

---

[5] See Adrian Vermeule. "Beyond Originalism." *The Atlantic*, March 31, 2020.

[6] Adrian Vermeule. *Common Good Constitutionalism: Recovering the Classical Legal Tradition.* (Cambridge, UK: Polity Press, 2022) at pg 95.

[7] Corey Robin. *The Reactionary Mind: Conservatism From Edmund Burke to Donald Trump.* (Oxford, UK: Oxford University Press, 2017).

[8] See Edmund Neill. *Conservatism.* (Cambridge, UK: Polity Press, 2021) at pgs 140–141.

[9] Adrian Vermeule. *Common Good Constitutionalism: Recovering the Classical Legal Tradition.* (Cambridge, UK: Polity Press, 2022) at pg 36.

In brief, the common good is, for the purposes of the constitutional lawyer, the flourishing of a well-ordered political community. The common good is unitary and indivisible, not an aggregation of individual utilities. In its temporal aspect it represents the highest felicity or happiness of the whole political community, which is also the highest good of the individuals comprising the community. To give this more specific content, I look to the precepts of legal justice in the classical law-to live honorably, to harm no one, and to give each one what is due to him in justice-and to the related *ragion de stato* tradition in early modern Europe, which articulates the central goods at which constitutionalism should aim. These goods include, in a famous trinity, peace, justice, and abundance, which I extrapolate to modern conditions to include various forms of health, safety, and economic security. I also elicit from the tradition the key principles of solidarity and subsidiarity. The largest point of the tradition is that public authority is both natural and legitimate-rather than intrinsically suspect, as one might infer from certain strands of the liberal tradition.

Interestingly, for a book entitled *Common Good Constitutionalism*, Vermeule offers very few arguments for common good constitutionalism in the book itself. He defines the common good in the first chapter, offers some examples of the "classical law" tradition in American law in the second, and then moves onto how one applies common good constitutionalism in the final one. There are a lot of declaratory statements backed by appeals to tradition, such as "in the classical account, a genuinely common good is a good that is unitary ('one in number') and capable of being shared without being diminished."[10] This is rather contestable; Aristotle if nothing else seemed aware that a plurality of regimes and mixed regimes existed which might be considered just, but recognized that all would have imperfections predicated on whether they focused on servicing the one, the few, or the many. But more importantly, Vermeuele offers nothing more than the quick example of a football team united for victory to argue for this notion of a unitary and aggregative good. It isn't even a particularly good example since it ignores the rather straightforward moral question, which should be obvious to a Schmittian, that who gets to be included in the moral community or not is extremely important. What is of unitary good for one football team is a loss for another, though I suppose for some that doesn't matter since they just

---

[10] Adrian Vermeule. *Common Good Constitutionalism: Recovering the Classical Legal Tradition.* (Cambridge, UK: Polity Press, 2022) at pg 28.

aren't part of the in-group. At other points Vermeule will make statements of such sweeping generality that no one could contest them since very few people have argued otherwise. Elsewhere in *Common Good Constitutionalism* he argues that "human flourishing, including the flourishing of individuals, is itself essentially, not merely contingently, dependent upon the flourishing o the political communities (including ruling authorities) within which humans are always born, found, and embedded."[11] Has any liberal thinker ever contested this? Locke, a common whipping boy of post-liberals, was clear about the need to exist the state of nature to establish a quasi-republican government? J.S. Mill, the expressive individualist par excellence, identified as a socialist committed to the principles of liberty, equality, and of course fraternity.[12] Finally, at points Vermeule simply doesn't bother offering any arguments at all. When discussing his own conception of rights, he simply insists that "constitutional concepts such as liberty and equality need not be given libertarian or originalist readings" and that "Dworkin had a bad theory of rights" with a future argument promised but given.[13] This turns out not to be an argument for why should embrace the "classical" or "common good" interpretation of rights, but merely a description of how one could interpret the constitution that way. Once again there is a declaration that "on the classical conception rights are *iura* (the plural of *ius*) because *ius* is justice-affording to each what is due to each."[14] He is contrasted with another thin account of the liberal tradition of rights but never defended on its merits; instead Vermeule goes right into applying the classical conception to relitigate a variety of cases to get the common good outcome he wants.

One suspects that Vermeuele is uninterested in systematically defending common good constitutionalism, except largely through its negations of liberalism, because doesn't see any need to. *Common Good Constitutionalism* is very different than *Law's Empire* in that Vermeuele is largely speaking to an audience convinced of the virtues of conservative approaches to law, but just needs a little push to abandon originalism and

---

[11] See Adrian Vermeule. *Common Good Constitutionalism: Recovering the Classical Legal Tradition.* (Cambridge, UK: Polity Press, 2022) at pg 29.

[12] See Mill, J.S. *Socialism.* (Ottawa, ON: East India Publishing Company, 2020).

[13] Adrian Vermeule. *Common Good Constitutionalism: Recovering the Classical Legal Tradition.* (Cambridge, UK: Polity Press, 2022) at pg 41.

[14] Adrian Vermeule. *Common Good Constitutionalism: Recovering the Classical Legal Tradition.* (Cambridge, UK: Polity Press, 2022) at pg 166.

get with a more muscular program. This makes it unnecessary to offer systematic arguments for common good constitutionalism; one need only present it as a "framework orientation."[15]

A Critique of Post-Liberal Jurisprudence

Perhaps this approach was inevitable since very few but the already converted are likely to find Vermeule's "framework" appealing. He makes it very clear that common good constitutionalism would reject "expansive abortion rights, sexual orientation and gender identity rights, and similar progressive programs" at both the domestic and international legal levels.[16] Freedom of speech should be subject to strict qualifications based on the "quality and moral worth" of public speech.[17] Unlike other Trumpy conservatives like Yoram Hazony, Vermeule is willing to be skeptical of not just liberalism but also democracy, which is "valuable only insofar as it contributes to the common good, and not otherwise." Democracy "in the modern sense of modern mass electoral democracy" is to have no "special privilege" in deciding which regimes can best advance the common good.[18] While Vermeule acknowledges that this will undoubtedly appear authoritarian to many liberals and progressives, the ordinary "subjects" of his preferred regime will not long mind even if the law runs against a person's "own perceptions of what is best for them."

Common-good constitutionalism does not suffer from a horror of political domination and hierarchy, because it sees that law is parental, a wise teacher and an inculcator of good habits. Just authority in rulers can be exercised for the good of subjects, if necessary even against the subjects' own perceptions of what is best for them—perceptions that may change over time anyway, as the law teaches, habituates, and re-forms them. Subjects will come to thank the ruler whose legal strictures, possibly experienced at first as coercive, encourage subjects to form more authentic desires for the

---

[15] Adrian Vermeule. *Common Good Constitutionalism: Recovering the Classical Legal Tradition.* (Cambridge, UK: Polity Press, 2022) at pg 35.

[16] Adrian Vermeule. *Common Good Constitutionalism: Recovering the Classical Legal Tradition.* (Cambridge, UK: Polity Press, 2022) at pg 129.

[17] Adrian Vermeule. "Beyond Originalism." *The Atlantic,* March 31, 2020.

[18] Adrian Vermeule. *Common Good Constitutionalism: Recovering the Classical Legal Tradition.* (Cambridge, UK: Polity Press, 2022 at pgs 47–48.

individual and common goods, better habits, and beliefs that better track and promote communal well-being.[19]

This tells us a lot about what prevents Vermuele from becoming the theocratic Dworkin he longs to be. For Dworkin, a key basis for legitimating the right of law to coercive authority was the extent to which it respected each citizen as an equal and took their rights to individual liberty seriously. This is aligned with the hermeneutic approach to argumentation Dworkin adopts, where the reasons for a given legal decision must be publicly justified to citizens who are ultimately equal partners in law's empire.[20] Vermeuelean paternalistic authoritarianism rejects this partnership notion of democracy and civic equality, and sees nothing wrong with a "mixed regime" where judicial elites will impose their conception of the common good on even those who disagree.[21] While Vermeuele thinks everyone will eventually "thank the ruler whose legal strictures, possible experienced at first as coercive, encourage subjects to form more authentic desires" I doubt that the liberals, LGBTQ individuals, women, religious minorities who will be marginalized by it will feel especially thankful.

This connects to a deeper objection to Vermeuelean paternalistic authoritarianism, which is its strangely decisionistic relativism. For Vermeuele "sacramental liberalism" is but one "political theology" among many "and that the behavior of liberal agents often cannot be adequately understood without this lens. Liberalism, on this view, is best understood as an imperfectly secularized offshoot of Christianity, whose main features are not only a notorious 'immanentist hypostasis of the eschaton' but an odd and distinctive mix of Pelagianism and Gnosticism."[22] While liberalism may celebrate a "festival" of reason, it is just as sacramental and liturgical as any other theological doctrine. This goes right down to the various idols worshipped by liberals.

---

[19] Adrian Vermeule. "Beyond Originalism." *The Atlantic*, March 31, 2020.

[20] See Ronald Dworkin. *Law's Empire*. (Cambridge, MA: Harvard University Press, 1986).

[21] Adrian Vermeule. *Common Good Constitutionalism: Recovering the Classical Legal Tradition*. (Cambridge, UK: Polity Press, 2022) at pg 47–48.

[22] Adrian Vermeule. "All Human Conflict is Ultimately Theological." *Church Life Journal*, July 26, 2019.

The basic liturgy of liberalism is the Festival of Reason, which in 1793 placed a Goddess of Reason (who may or may not have been a prostitute conscripted for the occasion, in one of the mocking double entendres of Providence) on the holy altar in the Church of Our Lady in Paris. The more the Enlightenment rejects the sacramental, the more compulsively it re-enacts its founding Festival, the dawning of rationality.[23]

As with Schmitt's own work, the effect of rhetorically stamping liberalism as just another political theology is to blur the difference between liberals and their reactionary opponents.[24] By caricaturing liberalism as any other theology to emerge from Christianity, and a heretical one at that, it undermines the argumentative claims of liberals to offer a rationally defensible theory of justice. Instead they are tribalistically offering their own God for worship and punishing or banishing those who don't bow at the altar. Given this, Vermeule has no need to comprehensively argue for common good constitutionalism since that would be as much of a waste of time as those who think they can offer a rationalistic defense of liberalism. The point is to demarcate the boundaries of various faith traditions, highlight the theological stakes at play, and then let them "conflict" until a winner comes to the fore. What is never stated in these agonistic ruminations is how, in such a context, it will ultimately be power-given a sublime coding as "authority"—that settles the issue. This has always made just this kind of agonism attractive to right-wing theocrats since it negates the requirement that we regard the most vulnerable as equal partners through facilitating a true elite's rise to absolutism through victory.

What is interesting about this is of course in part how, as with Schmitt, this agonistic vision of politics as a theological struggle between value systems that can only be settled through power has more in common with Nietzsche than Christ. This is true both at the level of value and epistemology. Fascinatingly, for all Vermeuele echoes many of the standard revanchist anxieties about the nihilism of liberal modernity his work Dworkin's undeniable commitment to the intellectual pursuit of objectivity and truth through carefully reasoned argumentation. This is especially odd given the philosophical traditions whose authority Vermeuele

---

[23] Adrian Vermeule. "Liturgy of Liberalism." *First Things,* January 2017.

[24] Carl Schmitt. *Political Theology.* (Chicago, IL: The University of Chicago Press, 2005).

relentlessly appeals to. There is nothing approximating a *Summa* or even a *Theology and Social Theory* or even the ontotheological musings of *Natural Law and Natural Right* in Vermeuele's oeuvre. Ergo leaving the foundation of his entire system looking like little more than ultra-modern Schmittian tinged theological decisionism. This is all that is left over when you flatten all epistemic and normative truths claims to various theological assertions whose validity only emerges from reification into authority by power. Given this it isn't clear how a legal system predicated on common good constitutionalism, enacting a political vision that is neither very common and certainly not good, could legitimately claim a right to obedience from citizens.

WILL POST-LIBERAL JURISPRUDENCE TAKE OFF?

Despite its lack of theoretical appeal Vermeule is absolutely correct about one thing. Now that conservatives control much of the American judiciary, there is nothing to keep them from pursuing a more muscular version of their now 50 year quest for a more unjust America.[25] Nothing, of course, except the fact that adopting such a transparently and sweepingly activist form of juristocratic rule would run contrary to the rhetorical and argumentative thrust of decades of conservative argumentation.[26] This includes from revered figures like Antonin Scalia and Robert Bork who often prided themselves on presenting originalism as a purely "neutral" way of interpreting the law which was not in itself ideologically motivated. While Vermeule, Deneen, and some others may be comfortable simply abandoning such pretenses to judicial impartiality and legislate from the bench it may well be a difficult pitch for conservatives lawyers accultured to a very different rhetoric.

Nonetheless there are signs that a shift is taking place within conservative legal thought to embrace the more muscular revanchism of post-liberal jurisprudence. The publication of Vermeule's *Common Good Constitutionalism* was greeted with a major symposium launched by the

---

[25] See Adam Cohen. *Supreme Inequality: The Supreme Courts 50 Year Battle For A More Unjust America.* (New York, NY: Penguin Books, 2020).

[26] See Steven Teles. *The Rise of the Conservative Legal Movement: The Battle for Control of the Law.* (Princeton, NJ: Princeton University Press, 2010) and Steven G. Calabresi. *Originalism: A Quarter-Century of Debate.* (Washington, DC: Regnery Publishing Inc, 2007).

Harvard Journal of Law and Public Policy in conjunction with the Federalist Society. In attendance were a variety of esteemed legal scholars, along with internationally important Judges like James C. Ho and Justice Bradley W. Miller.[27] There is evidence that younger and more radical conservative lawyers and law students are at least open to abandoning originalism for the more assertive approach to jurisprudence offered by figures like Vermeule and Deneen. As Ian Ward noted, commenting on the symposia, while supporters of post-liberal justice remain "a distinct minority within the broader conservative ecosystem, but as the youthfulness of the audience in the Revolution Room suggested, their ideas have made particular inroads among young conservative lawyers and law students."[28]

What is most likely to occur is that conservative jurists would adopt variations of common good constitutionalism in all but name while retaining the rhetorical trappings or originalist objectivity and neutrality. There is nothing that says one needs to be overt about a turn to post-liberal judicial activism. Or that one couldn't present even militantly revanchist judgments as agonistic reprisals against liberal overreach from the bench. The latter would be especially well suited to the modern American conservative movement. At a rhetorical level Republican politicians like Ron DeSantis have mastered the art of declaring "its textbook judicial activism when courts abandon [a] limited judicial role and legislate from the bench" while denying that Judges need not "avoid issuing consequential rulings at all" since this would create a "one-way racket, whereby leftist judges issues sweeping rulings untethered to the law and constitution while judicial conservatives accept flawed precedents and shy away from faithfully applying the constitution when doing so has a significant impact." Indeed DeSantis wants Judges who would "relish defying" liberal law.[29]

In some respects the turn to a more muscular post-liberal jurisprudence has been a long time coming for precisely the reasons Dworkin and his dark counterpart Vermeule have stressed. The cruder variations of

---

[27] *CGC Symposium*, October 29, 2022. https://www.harvard-jlpp.com/symposia/cgc-symposium/.

[28] See Ian Ward. "Critics Call It Theocratic and Authoritarian. Young Conservatives Call It an Exciting New Legal Theory." *Politico*, December 9, 2022.

[29] See Ron De Santis. *The Courage to Be Free: Florida's Blueprint for America's Revival.* (New York, NY: Broadside Books, 2023) at pgs 100–101.

the separation thesis which suppose Judges evade principled interpretations of what law should be for a technical and neutral insistence on what it is was never a viable claim. That conservatives are now accepting that is intellectually gratifying, but strategically rich given their long insistence on the opposite. The question then becomes how to confront this effectively. And here is where Dworkin and Dworkineanism can be such a vital resource to legal liberals.

Dworkin Against Postliberal Justice

Post-liberalism has a variety of appeals. At the present post-liberals are capable of presenting themselves as simultaneously both a counter-cultural movement, defying the powers that be, and being committed to a restorative project that will establish order through power and call it authority. This makes it attractive to a certain kind of reactionary resentiment which simultaneously sees itself as victimized by oppressive liberal forces and a potential elite in waiting whose deserved power and status has for too long been denied.[30] Patrick Deneen's recent *Regime Change*, which calls for the replacement of a neoliberal elite with a conservative "ruling class" committed to the "common good" and swept to victory by aristopopulism (aristocratic populism) is representative here.[31]

To the extent liberals and democrats should eschew a politics of resentment this is obviously a weak point. But the more basic source of post-liberalism's appeal is its superficial moral seriousness and clarity of purpose. Post-liberals survey our present and vacillate between describing it as liberationist and nihilistically permissive, increasingly authoritarian and domineering, or some immanent combination of the two. Against this they promise that a return to actual authoritarianism would at least be preferable, since its clarity of moral purpose could curb the excesses of liberationist philosophy and inoculate against hypocritical overreach when the consequences of driving for absolute freedom come home to roost. Of course this requires maximally empowering the political freedom of their preferred elite, while disempowering and resubordinating the masses. For their own good of course.

---

[30] See Wendy Brown. *In the Ruins of Neoliberalism: The Rise of Antidemocratic Politics in the West.* (New York, NY: Columbia University Press, 2019).

[31] See Patrick Deneen. *Regime Change: Toward a Postliberal Future.* (New York, NY: Sentinel Press, 2023).

Much of this is based upon very old reactionary critiques of liberalism which see it as breaking apart ordered societies defined by hierarchical complementarity, while appealing to Hirschman's perversity rhetoric to suggest liberals would just install new and worse hierarchies than what came before. Nevertheless it is an objection that routinely resurfaces because it is absolutely the case that where liberal democracies stop committing to their basic principles with integrity, it opens the door to reactionary criticisms which promise that a stern hand can better tend to the "people." For decades now neoliberal and other right-wing forms of liberalism have failed to advance a politics which respects the equal worth of all lives and empowers each individual to take special responsibility for their own. Instead we've seen a movement toward plutocratic rule and deepening inequality, often advanced in the name of upholding "liberal" principles for corporations like Citizens United. In a word it isn't liberalism that has failed, it is liberals.

Dworkin's philosophy and jurisprudence offers us a way to respond to post-liberalism which is unapologetically committed to a muscular liberal egalitarianism. To the extent post-liberals are current to stress that a kind of communitarian meaning has been lost in the neoliberal era the solution shouldn't be a retreat into authoritarian aristopopulism. Instead we need to recover the ideal of liberal societies as partnership democracies committed to securing for all their members lives of dignity and equal respect. This can in part be accomplished through aligning lawyer and Judges with his approach to the constitution and recovers the project of taking rights seriously, rather than rolling them back as the conservative Supreme Court has been attempting for decades now.[32] There are good reasons why this would be viable in our current moment.

The first and more trivial is generational. Rather than becoming less liberal and adapting to conservative authoritarianism, polls suggest American Millennials and Zoomers will be and remain among the most progressive generations.[33] This suggests a context where intelligent established and incoming legal practitioners would be engaged by a substantively progressive approach to jurisprudence which goes beyond the "trashing" common to critical legal studies—even if it will have to

---

[32] See Adam Cohen. *Supreme Inequality: The Supreme Courts 50 Year Battle For A More Unjust America.* (New York, NY: Penguin Books, 2020).

[33] See Kim Parker, Nikki Graf, and Ruth Igielnik. "Generation Z Looks a Lot Like Millennials on Key Social and Political Issues." *Pew Research Center*, January 17, 2019.

draw extensively on CLS' theories of power to compensate for analytical and empirical gaps in Dworkin's sometimes idealized analysis. One technique conservative jurists have been very effective at is presenting themselves as engaged in ideas and sweeping moral questions, which has long helped make legal conservatism appealing to young lawyers.[34] This always went beyond just critiquing legal liberalism and offering alternatives. A modified Dworkinian jurisprudence could serve as a theoretical framework for dynamic progressivism which similarly engages both the passions and the head.

But the more important reason for embracing Dworkinean liberalism is, of course, the principled one. To the extent we believe in the objectivity and truth of liberal justice, it is impossible to see post-liberal authoritarianism as anything but patently unjust. Especially toward the sexual and gender minorities whom post-liberals go out of their way to condemn, and whose hard fought victories were among the few achievements of American legal liberalism in the twenty-first century. Replacing plutocratic neoliberalism and its fig leaf egalitarianism with transparent aristocratic rule is exchanging Coriolanus for Iago. It would entail interpreting the principles of the American constitution in manner so lacking integrity heir liberal and egalitarian core was dropped in such establish a revanchist "regime" where all citizens were not even nominally equal partners, but superior and subordinate, rulers and ruled. Not "we the people" but aristopopulists ruling from on high while promising to take the odd shop class to tour blue collar life.

CONCLUSION

Without dignity our lives are only blinks of duration. But if we manage to lead a good life well, we create something more. We write a subscript to our mortality. We make our lives tiny diamonds in the cosmic sands.
    Ronald Dworkin

A narrow moral imagination limits itself to concern only with one's own life, or at most those close by. At its worst a narrow liberalism can

---

[34] See Steven Teles. *The Rise of the Conservative Legal Movement: The Battle for Control of the Law*. (Princeton, NJ: Princeton University Press, 2010).

devolve in such a direction, turning to atomism and banal hedonistic gratification. In such moments it makes all the sense in the world to believe that there are no others, only individuals and they must look after themselves. Faced with the finitude of human existence, we can only say with Ayn Rand that when I do so too does the world cease to exist. But at its best the liberal imagination comes to regard all life as precious, starting from its own and extending outwards to encompass concern for all that were, are, and will be; seeing all as unique and contributing partners in that most ambitious of all chain novels.

In his final works Dworkin described himself as, like Einstein, at once not a believer and yet a very religious man.[35] This is because for all he struggled to accept a belief in the monotheistic God, he nevertheless approached human existence with a degree of moral seriousness that testified to both its intrinsic value and the responsibility to lead a good life. Embodying his own philosophy with integrity, Dworkin lived a very good life indeed. But without justice, the first virtue of social institutions, millions of his fellow citizens will struggle to do the same. What they need are liberals who will no longer accept such a situation. The arc of the moral universe is long but it bends toward justice.

---

[35] See Ronald Dworkin. *Justice for Hedgehogs*. (Cambridge, MA: Harvard University Press, 2010).

BIBLIOGRAPHY

BOOKS AND JOURNAL ARTICLES

Anderson, Elizabeth. *Private Government: How Employers Rule Our Lives (And Why We Don't Talk About It)*. (Princeton, NJ: Princeton University Press, 2017).

Anghie, Antony. "Francisco de Vittoria and the Colonial Origins of International Law." *Social Legal Studies*, Vol 5, 1996.

Backhouse, Constance. *Colour-Coded: A Legal History of Racism in Canada*. (Toronto, ON: University of Toronto Press, 1999).

Bork, Robert. *Coercing Virtue: The Worldwide Rule of Judges*. (Toronto, ON: Vintage Canada, 2002).

Bork, Robert. "The End of Democracy? Our Judicial Oligarchy" in *First Things*, November 1996.

Brennan, Jason. *Against Democracy*. (Princeton, NJ: Princeton University Press, 2016).

Brown, Wendy. *In the Ruins of Neoliberalism: The Rise of Antidemocratic Politics in the West*. (New York, NY: Columbia University Press, 2019).

Calabresi, Steven G. *Originalism: A Quarter-Century of Debate*. (Washington, DC: Regnery Publishing Inc, 2007).

Cohen, Adam. *Supreme Inequality: The Supreme Courts 50 Year Battle for a More Unjust America*. (New York, NY: Penguin Books, 2020).

Cunningham, Frank. *The Political Thought of C.B MacPherson: Contemporary Applications*. (Cham, SW: Palgrave MacMillan, 2019).

© The Author(s), under exclusive license to Springer Nature Switzerland AG 2023
L. A. Jacobs and M. McManus, *Against Post-Liberal Courts and Justice*, Palgrave Studies in Classical Liberalism,
https://doi.org/10.1007/978-3-031-45347-2

Dahl, Robert. *How Democratic is the American Constitution.* (New Haven, CN: Yale University Press, 2003).

Dahl, Robert. *On Democracy.* (New Haven, CN: Yale University Press, 2000).

Dawson, Hannah and de Dijn, Annelien. *Rethinking Liberty Before Liberalism.* (Cambridge, UK: Cambridge University Press, 2023).

Deneen, Patrick. "After Liberalism: Can We Imagine a Humane, Post-Liberal Future?" *Religion and Ethics*, December 2014. http://www.abc.net.au/rel igion/articles/2014/12/11/4146762.htm.

Deneen, Patrick. *Conserving America: Essays on Present Discontents.* (South Bend, IN: St. Augustine Press, 2016).

Deneen, Patrick. *Democratic Faith.* (Princeton, NJ: Princeton University Press, 2005).

Deneen, Patrick. "How Will Future Historians Treat Same-Sex Marriage." *The Public Discourse*, July 10, 2013.

Patrick Deneen. *Regime Change: Toward a Postliberal Future.* (New York, NY: Sentinel Press, 2023).

Deneen, Patrick. "Unsustainable Liberalism." *First Things*, August 2012.

Deneen, Patrick. *Why Liberalism Failed.* (New Haven, CN: Yale University Press, 2018).

DeSantis, Ron. *The Courage to Be Free: Florida's Blueprint for America's Revival.* (New York, NY: Broadside Books, 2023).

Devlin, Patrick. "The Enforcement of Morals." *The Maccabean Lecture in Jurisprudence*, March 1959.

Douzinas, Costas. *The End of Human Rights: Critical Thought at the Turn of the Century.* (Portland, OR: Hart Publishing, 2000).

Douzinas, Costas. "Seven Theses on Human Rights (Desire)" *Critical Legal Thinking*, June 3, 2013.

Douzinas, Costas. "What Are Human Rights?" *The Guardian*, March 18, 2009.

Dworkin, Ronald. "Bork's Jurisprudence." *The University of Chicago Law Review*, Vol 57, 1990.

Dworkin, Ronald "The Decision that Threatens Democracy." *The New York Review of Books*, May 13, 2010.

Dworkin, Ronald. *Freedom's Law: The Moral Reading of the American Constitution.* (Cambridge, MA: Harvard University Press, 1997).

Dworkin, Ronald. "Hard Cases." *Harvard Law Review*, Vol 88, 1975.

Dworkin, Ronald. "Hart's Postscript and the Character of Political Philosophy." *Oxford Journal of Legal Studies*, Vol 24, No 1, 2004.

Dworkin, Ronald "Interview on the Constitution." *Philosophy Overdose*, October 1, 2022. https://www.youtube.com/watch?v=VmjloTrxh1M&t=903s.

Dworkin, Ronald. *Is Democracy Possible Here?: Principles for a New Political Debate.* (Princeton, NJ: Princeton University Press, 2006).

Dworkin, Ronald. "Is There Truth In Interpretation? Law, Literature, and History." *Library of Congress*, December 17, 2009 at https://www.youtube.com/watch?v=742JyiqLhuk.

Dworkin, Ronald. *Justice for Hedgehogs*. (Cambridge, MA. Harvard University Press, 2010).

Dworkin, Ronald. *Law's Empire*. (Cambridge, MA: Harvard University Press, 1986).

Dworkin, Ronald. *Life's Dominion: An Argument About Abortion, Euthanasia, and Individual Freedom*. (New York, NY: Vintage Books, 1994).

Dworkin, Ronald. "Lord Devlin and the Enforcement of Morals." *The Yale Law Journal*, Vol 75, No 6, 1966.

Dworkin, Ronald. *A Matter of Principle*. (Cambridge, MA: Harvard University Press, 1985).

Dworkin, Ronald. "A Model of Rules." *The University of Chicago Law Review*, Vol 35, 1967.

Dworkin, Ronald. "Objectivity and Truth: You'd Better Believe It." *Philosophy and Public Affairs*, Vol 25, 1996.

Dworkin, Ronald. "Rawls and the Law." *Fordham Law Review*, Vol 72, 2004.

Dworkin, Ronald. *Sovereign Virtue: The Theory and Practice of Equality*. (Cambridge, MA: Harvard University Press, 2002).

Dworkin, Ronald. *Taking Rights Seriously*. (Cambridge, MA: Harvard University Press, 1977).

Dworkin, Ronald. "The Decision That Threatens Democracy." *New York Review of Books*, May 13, 2010.

Dyzenhaus, David. "Hobbes and the Legitimacy of Law." *Law and Philosophy*, Vol 20, 2001.

Dyzenhaus, David. "Liberalism After the Fall: Schmitt, Rawls, and the Problem of Justification." *Philosophy and Social Criticism*, Vol 22, 1996.

Edmundson, William A. *John Rawls: Reticent Socialist*. (Cambridge, UK: Cambridge University Press, 2017).

Eatwell, Roger and Goodwin, Matthew. *National Populism and the Revolt Against Liberal Democracy*. (London, UK: Penguin Books, 2018).

Ely, John. *Democracy and Distrust: A Theory of Judicial Review*. (Cambridge, MA: Harvard University Press, 1981).

Ewald, William. "Unger's Philosophy: A Critical Legal Study." *The Yale Law Journal*, Vol 97, 1988.

Ewick, Patricia and Silbey, Susan. *The Common Place of Law: Stories from Everyday Life*. (Chicago, IL. University of Chicago Press, 1998).

Ewick, Patricia and Silbey, Susan. "Conformity, Contestation, and Resistance: An Account of Legal Consciousness." *New England Law Review*, Vol 26, 1992.

Finnis, John. "The Critical Legal Studies Movement." *The American Journal of Jurisprudence*, Vol 30, 1985.

Finnis, John. "Law, Morality, and Sexual Orientation" in John Corvino. *Same Sex: Debating the Ethics, Science, and Culture of Homosexuality.* (Lanham, NY: Rowman and Littlefield, 1997).

Finnis, John. *Natural Law and Natural Rights: Second Edition.* (Oxford, UK. Oxford University Press, 2011).

Foucault, Michel. *The Archaeology of Knowledge,* trans. A.M Sheridan Smith. (London and New York, NY: Routledge, 2007).

Fuller, Lon. *The Morality of Law: Revised Edition.* (New Haven, CN: Yale University Press, 1969).

Fuller, Lon. "Positivism and Fidelity to the Law: A Reply to Professor Hart." *Harvard Law Review,* Vol 71, 1958.

Gabel, Peter. "Critical Legal Studies as Spiritual Practice." *Pepperdine Law Review,* Vol 36, 2012.

Genn, Hazel, *Paths to Justice: What People Do and Think about Going to Law,* (Oxford, UK: Hart Publishing, 1999).

Gilens, Martin and Page, Benjamin I. "Testing Theories of American Politics: Elites, Interests Groups, and Average Citizens." *Perspectives on Politics,* Vol 12, 2014.

Guinier, Lani. *The Tyranny of the Majority: Fundamental Freedoms in Representative Democracy.* (New York, NY: The Free Press, 1995).

Habermas, Jürgen. *The Theory of Communicative Action Volume Two: Lifeworld and System-A Critique of Functionalist Reason,* trans. Thomas McCarthy. (Boston, MA: Beacon Press, 1985).

Hagglund, Martin. *This Life: Secular Faith and Spiritual Freedom.* (London, UK: Penguin Pantheon Books, 2019).

Hamilton, Alexander and Madison, James and Jay, John. *The Federalist Papers.* (New York, NY: Signet, 2003).

Hart, H.L.A. *The Concept of Law: Second Edition.* (Oxford, UK: Oxford University Press, 1997).

Hart, H.L.A. *Essays in Jurisprudence and Philosophy.* (Oxford, UK: Oxford University Press, 1984).

Hart, H.L.A. *Law, Liberty, and Morality.* (Stanford, CA: Stanford University Press, 1963).

Hart, H.L.A. "Positivism and the Separation of Law and Morals." *Harvard Law Review,* Vol 71, 1958.

Hayek, FA. *Law, Legislation and Liberty.* (Chicago, IL: University of Chicago Press, 2022).

Hazony Yoram. *Conservatism: A Rediscovery.* (Washington, DC: Regnery Press, 2022).

Hazony, Yoram. "Conservative Democracy: Liberal Principles Have Brought Us a Dead End." *First Things,* January 2019.

Hazony, Yoram. "The Challenge of Marxism." *Quillette,* August 16, 2020.

Hazony, Yoram. *The Virtue of Nationalism.* (New York, NY: Basic Books, 2018).

Hazony, Yoram. "Why National Conservatism?" *National Conservatism*, July 15, 2019. https://www.youtube.com/watch?v=4cpyd1OqHJU&t=1725s.

Hendricks, Obery. *Christians Against Christianity: How Right-Wing Evangelicals Are Destroying Our Nation and Our Faith.* (Boston, MA: Beacon Press, 2021).

Hirschman, Albert O. *The Rhetoric of Reaction: Perversity, Futility, Jeopardy.* (Cambridge, MA: The Belknap Pres of Harvard University Press, 1991).

Howe, Irving. "Liberalism and Socialism: Articles of Conciliation?" *Dissent Magazine*, Winter 1977.

Hutchinson, Allan. *Evolution and the Common Law.* (Cambridge, UK: Cambridge University Press, 2005).

Hutchinson, Allan. "Indiana Dworkin and Law's Empire." *Yale Law Journal*, Vol 96, 1987.

Hutchinson, Allan. *Is Eating People Wrong?: Great Legal Cases And How They Shaped The World.* (New York, NY: Cambridge University Press, 2011).

Hutchinson, Allan. "Judges and Politics: An Essay from Canada." *Supreme Court Law Review*, Vol 25, 2004.

Hutchinson, Allan. "A Poetic Champion Composes: Unger (Not) On Ecology and Women." *The University of Toronto Law Journal*, Vol 40, 1990.

Hutchinson, Allan. *Waiting for C.O.R.A.F.* (Toronto, ON: University of Toronto Press, 1995).

Kelman, M.G. "Trashing." *Stanford Law Review*, Vol 36, 1984.

Kennedy, Duncan. "The Critique of Rights in Critical Legal Studies" in Janet Halley and Wendy Brown. *Left Legalism/Left Critique.* (Durham, NC: Duke University Press, 2002).

Kennedy, Duncan. *A Critique of Adjudication (Fin De Siècle).* (Cambridge, MA. Harvard University Press, 1997).

Kennedy, Duncan. "Form and Substance in Private Law Adjudication." *Harvard Law Review*, Vol 89, 1976.

Khurshid, Salman and Malik, Lokendra and Rodriguez-Blanco, Veronica. *Dignity in the Legal and Political Philosophy of Ronald Dworkin.* (Oxford, UK: Oxford University Press, 2018).

Koskeniemmi, Martti. *The Gentle Civilizer of Nations: The Rise and Fall of International Law 1870–1960.* (Cambridge, UK: Cambridge University Press, 2001).

Lawler, Peter. *Stuck with Virtue: The American Individual and Our Biotechnological Future.* (Wilmington, DE: ISI Books, 2005).

Losurdo, Domenico. *Liberalism: A Counter-History.* (London, UK: Verso Press, 2014).

MacIntyre, Alasdair. *After Virtue-A Study in Moral Theory: Third Edition* (Notre Dame, IN: University of Notre-Dame Press, 2007).

MacIntyre, Alasdair. *Marcuse.* (Roermond, NL: Fontana, 1970).

MacIntyre, Alasdair. *Marxism and Christianity.* (Notre Dame, Indiana: University of Notre Dame Press, 2003).

Macintyre, Alasdair. "The Virtues, the Unity of a Human Life, and the Concept of a Tradition" in Michael Sandel. *Liberalism and Its Critics.* (New York, NY: New York University Press, 1984).

MacIntyre, Alasdair. *Whose Justice, Which Rationality?* (Notre Dame, IN: University of Notre-Dame Press, 1989).

MacKinnon, Catherine. "The Liberal State." Printed in David Dyzenhaus, Sophia Reibetanz Moreau, and Arthur Ripstein. *Law and Morality-Readings in Legal Philosophy: Third Edition.* (Toronto, Ontario: University of Toronto Press, 2007).

MacKinnon, Catherine. "Points Against Postmodernism." *Chicago-Kent Law Review*, Vol 25, June 2000.

MacKinnon, Catherine and Dworkin, Ronald. "Pornography-An Exchange." *New York Review of Books*, October 21, 1993.

MacKinnon, Catherine. "Rape, Genocide and Women's Human Rights." *Harvard Women's Law Journal*, Vol 17, 1994.

MacKinnon, Catherine. *Towards a Feminist Theory of the State.* (Cambridge, MA: Harvard University Press, 1989).

MacPherson, C.B. *The Political Theory of Possessive Individualism: Hobbes to Locke.* (Oxford, UK: Oxford University Press, 2011).

McManus, Matthew. "A Critical Legal Conception of Human Dignity." *Journal of Human Rights*, Online, 2019.

McManus, Matthew. *The Emergence of Postmodernity at the Intersection of Liberalism, Capitalism, and Secularism.* (Cham, Switzerland: Palgrave MacMillan, 2022).

Mill, J.S. *Socialism.* (Ottawa, ON: East India Publishing Company, 2020).

Morton, F.L and Knopff, Rainer. *The Charter Revolution and the Court Party.* (Toronto, ON: University of Toronto Press, 2000).

Moyn, Samuel. *Not Enough: Human Rights in an Unequal World.* (Cambridge, MA: Belknap Press of Harvard University Press, 2019).

Moyn, Samuel. "The Court is Not Your Friend." *Dissent Magazine*, Winter 2020.

Mullender, Richard. "Ronald Dworkin: Justice for Hedgehogs." *Philosophy in Review*, Vol XXXIV, 2014.

Parker, Kim and Graf, Nikki and Igielnik, Ruth. "Generation Z Looks a Lot Like Millennials on Key Social and Political Issues." *Pew Research Center*, January 17, 2019.

Petter, Andrew. *The Politics of the Charter: The Illusive Promise of Constitutional Rights.* (Toronto, ON: The University of Toronto Press, 2010).

Piketty, Thomas. *Capital and Ideology*, trans. Arthur Goldhammer. (Cambridge, MA: Harvard University Press, 2020).

Rawls, John. "The Idea of Public Reason Revisited." *The University of Chicago Law Review*, Vol 64, 1997.

Rawls, John. *Justice as Fairness: A Restatement*. (Cambridge, MA. The Belknap Press of Harvard University Press, 2001).

Rawls, John. *The Law of Peoples: With the "Idea of Public Reason Revisited."* (United States: Harvard University Press, 2001).

Rawls, John. *Lectures on the History of Political Philosophy*. (Cambridge, MA: The Belknap Press of Harvard University Press, 2008).

Rawls, John. *Political Liberalism* (New York, NY: Columbia University Press, 1993).

Rawls, John. *A Theory of Justice: Revised Edition*. (Cambridge, MA: Harvard University Press, 1999).

Razack, Sherene. *The Eviction of Muslims from Western Law and Politics*. (Toronto, ON: University of Toronto Press, 2008).

Reno, R.R. *Resurrecting the Idea of Christian Society*. (Washington, DC: Regnery Faith, 2016).

Reno, R.R. *Return of the Strong Gods: Nationalism, Populism, and the Future of the West*. (Washington, DC: Regnery Faith, 2019).

Robin, Corey. *The Reactionary Mind: Conservatism from Edmund Burke to Donald Trump*. (Oxford, UK: Oxford University Press, 2017).

Russell, Kathryn. "A Value-Theoretic Approach to Childbirth" in Rosemary Hennessy and Chrys Ingraham. *Materialist Feminist: A Reader in Class, Difference, and Women's Lives*. (New York, NY: Routledge Press, 1997).

Sandel, Michael. *Liberalism and the Limits of Justice: Second Edition*. (Cambridge, UK: Cambridge University Press, 1998).

Scalia, Antonin. *A Matter of Interpretation: Federal Courts and the Law*. (Princeton, NJ: Princeton Paperbacks, 1997).

Schlag, Pierre. "The Empty Circles of Liberal Justification." *Michigan Law Review*, Vol 96, 1997.

Schlag, Pierre. "Normativity and the Politics of Form." *University of Pennsylvania Law Review*, Vol 139, 1991.

Schlag, Pierre. *The Enchantment of Reason*. (Durham, NC: Duke University Press, 1998).

Schmitt, Carl. *The Concept of the Political: Expanded Edition*. (Chicago, IL. The University of Chicago Press, 2007).

Schmitt, Carl. *Constitutional Theory*, trans. Jeffrey Seitzer. (Durham, NC. Duke University Press, 2008).

Schmitt, Carl. *Legality and Legitimacy*, trans. Jeffrey Seitzer. (Chicago, IL: University of Chicago Press, 2004).

Schmitt, Carl. *The Leviathan in the State Theory of Thomas Hobbes.* (Chicago, IL. The University of Chicago Press, 2008).

Schmitt, Carl. *The Nomos of the Earth in the International Law of Jus Publicum Europeaum.* (Candor, NY: Telos Press, 2006).

Schmitt, Carl. *Political Theology.* (Chicago, IL. The University of Chicago Press, 2005).

Sen, Amartya. *The Idea of Justice.* (Cambridge, MA: Harvard University Press, 2009).

Shapiro, Scott. *Legality.* (Cambridge, MA: Belknap Press of Harvard University Press, 2011).

Teles, Steven. *The Rise of the Conservative Legal Movement: The Battle for Control of the Law.* (Princeton, NJ: Princeton University Press, 2010).

Thomson, Judis Jarvis. "A Defense of Abortion." *Philosophy and Public Affairs,* Vol 1, No 1.

Toth, Csaba. "Full text of Viktor Orbán's speech at Băile Tuşnad (Tusnádfürdő) of 26 July 2014." *The Budapest Beacon,* July 29, 2014.

Traub, James. "Its Time for the Elites To Rise Up Against the Ignorant Masses." *Foreign Policy,* June 28, 2016.

Tully, James. *Strange Multiplicity: Constitutionalism in An Age of Diversity.* (Cambridge, UK: Cambridge University Press, 1995).

Unger, Roberto. *The Critical Legal Studies Movement: Another Time, Another Task.* (Cambridge, MA. Harvard University Press, 2015).

Unger, Roberto. *Knowledge and Politics.* (New York, NY: The Free Press, 1975).

Unger, Roberto. *What Should the Left Propose?* (London, UK: Verso Press, 2005).

Vermeule, Adrian. "All Human Conflict is Ultimately Theological." *Church Life Journal,* July 26, 2019.

Vermeule, Adrian. "Beyond Originalism." *The Atlantic,* March 31, 2020.

Vermeule, Adrian. *Common Good Constitutionalism: Recovering the Classical Legal Tradition.* (Cambridge, UK: Polity Press, 2022).

Vermeule, Adrian. "Liturgy of Liberalism." *First Things,* January 2017.

Ward, Ian. "Critics Call It Theocratic and Authoritarian. Young Conservatives Call It an Exciting New Legal Theory." *Politico,* December 9, 2022.

Ward, Ian. *Introduction to Critical Legal Theory: Second Edition.* (New York, NY: Routledge-Cavendish, 2004).

Williams, Bernard. *Morality: An Introduction to Ethics.* (Cambridge, UK: Cambridge University Press, 2012).

Wittgenstein, Ludwig. *Philosophical Investigations,* trans. G.E.M Anscombe, P.M.S Hacker and Joachim Schulte. (Oxford, UK: Blackwell Publishing, 2001).

Wolin, Sheldon. *Fugitive Democracy and Other Essays.* (Princeton, NJ: Princeton University Press, 2016).

CASES

Citizens United v Federal Election Commission, No. 08-205, 558 U.S. 310 (2010).

Dobbs v. Jackson Women's Health Organization, No. 19-1392, 597 U.S (2022).

Planned Parenthood v. Casey, 505 U.S. 833 (1992).

Rucho v. Common Cause, No. 18-422, 588 U.S. (2019).

INDEX

Printed in the USA
CPSIA information can be obtained
at www.ICGtesting.com
LVHW021214080224
771299LV00004B/116